KING BHUMIBOL

and the Thai Royal Family in Lausanne

KING BHUMIBOL
and the Thai Royal Family in Lausanne

Recollections of HM King Rama IX's Tutor
assembled by
Lysandre C. Séraïdaris

*The publication of this book
has been made possible
through the generosity of
Tetra Pak (Thailand) Limited.*

The illustrations of this book are from the private collection of the author, unless otherwise specified.

Any reproduction of this book, even partial, is not permitted without written approval by the author.

This book under the title
Le Roi Bhumibol et la Famille Royale de Thaïlande à Lausanne
was originally published in French by
Éditions Slatkine, Geneva, Switzerland.
ISBN 978-2-8321-0539-9

Printed and bound in Thailand by Sirivatana Interprint Public Co.,Ltd.

ISBN 978-616-348-428-4
© Lysandre C. Séraïdaris 2012

CONTENTS

PREFACES

    Mr Daniel Brélaz   13

    Thanpuying Boonruen Choonhavan   17

    HE Khun Khwankeo Vajarodaya   19

PROLOGUE   21

SIMPLIFIED GENEALOGY OF THE ROYAL FAMILY   32

FIRST PART
MEMORIES OF THE TUTOR

1	The Future Tutor	37
2	Historic Encounter	51
3	Vadhana Villa	57
4	Life at Home	71
5	Temporary Return to the Kingdom	97
6	Return to Studious Life in Switzerland	121
7	Tragedy at the Palace	149
8	Return to Lausanne to finish Studies	177
9	Automotive Interlude	187

10	Role of the Personal Pages	215
11	King Rama IX	223
12	Farewell Lausanne	247
13	Return to Thailand and Beginning of Reign	249
14	The Royal Projects, Masterpieces of the King	271
15	Diplomatic Visits and Leisure Stay	285
16	The Tutor's Retirement	317
17	A Great Lady leaves Lausanne	337
18	The Tutor's Last Moments	345
19	HRH Princess Galyani Vadhana	353

SECOND PART
PERENNIALITY OF PRIVILEGED RELATIONSHIPS WITH LAUSANNE AND THE COUNTRY OF VAUD

20	The Royal Pavilion offered to the City of Lausanne	379
21	The *Confrérie du Guillon* received in Bangkok	405
22	Lausanne – Bangkok, Sister Cities	423

EPILOGUE	431
ACKNOWLEDGEMENTS	433
INDEX	435

PREFACES

I first came to know of Cléon Séraïdaris through his son, Lysandre. Not long after I became Mayor of Lausanne, Lysandre and I worked together to strengthen the excellent relationship that existed between Thailand and Lausanne and we initiated a new project to improve these relations for the future.

During several months of collaboration with Lysandre I was able to gauge the exceptional distinction which had been bestowed on his father Cléon, tutor of the Kings Rama VIII and Rama IX, who came to Lausanne with their mother and sister, at a decisive period of their childhood, to pursue their studies.

His Majesty King Rama IX left Lausanne the year after my birth, in 1951. His brother, HM King Rama VIII had spent twelve years living there, while his sister and his mother resided in the region more than fifty years.

I therefore discovered during my various encounters, firstly with the Grand Chamberlain, and later when I was honoured with an audience with his Majesty King Rama IX, a whole universe which shared a common destiny with my town for more than a decade whose key was Cléon Seraïdaris.

The older people of Lausanne still remember having come across the Royal Family, perfectly integrated into our ways and traditions, in the streets of the city.

It is to remind the people of Lausanne today of this remarkable atmosphere of understanding that the City of Lausanne has been particularly pleased to welcome the King's gift, in the form of a magnificent Thai Pavilion which was installed in Denantou Park, near the Royal Family's former Lausanne residence.

The Pavilion, inaugurated on 17 March 2009 by Her Royal Highness Princess Maha Chakri Sirindhorn, renews and reinforces the links between Lausanne and Thailand.

It is the testimony of the birth of these bonds which is recounted in this work.

Daniel Brélaz
Mayor of Lausanne

Thanpuying Boonruen Choonhavan is the niece of HRH Princess Mahidol, HM the King's Mother.

She is also the widower of HE General Chartchai Choonhavan who was for a long time a close advisor to HM the King, then Thai Ambassador to Switzerland from 1968 to 1972, and became the 17th Prime Minister of the Thai Government from 1990 to 1994.

Thanpuying Boonruen Choonhavan was also the President of the Association of Thai alumni in Switzerland from 1949 to 2010.

This work recounting the career and close role to the Thai Royal Family of Cléon Séraïdaris is the missing component in understanding the childhood of our two Kings brought up so far away from our Kingdom.

The people of Thailand will be fascinated to find out how Cléon, a young lawyer, having gone to the same school and the same university as our King, had the privilege of being his private tutor. Cléon was deeply respected by His Majesty the King for his thorough academic knowledge and standards, for his loyalty and uncompromising commitment to the Royal Family throughout his career.

I was pleasantly surprised to find contributions to this narration by the twin brothers, Kaewkhwan and Khwankeo Vajarodaya, who from their childhood have been inseparable from the history of the Royal Family both in Switzerland and Thailand and hold most prestigious posts within the Royal Household.

My late husband and I had a very warm relationship with Cléon and it is an honour for me to contribute a preface for this historic work.

Thanpuying Boonruen Choonhavan

Writing a preface is a sensitive task. One has to know the author, the subject matter, the personalities within and have a view of likely readers.

In this case I have known the author since his birth. My career close to the King allows me to recognize the accuracy of the story. The readers are simply all the Thais attached as they are to the monarchy and the Royal Family. The people of Switzerland and all friends of Thailand will find interest not only in this personal story but the history of Thailand and its institutions.

We have long awaited an authoritative work such as this to allow us to better appreciate the intellectual life our monarch King Bhumibol who has been conscious, since his youth, of the importance of education in promoting economic growth in the Kingdom.

We are fortunate that His Majesty King Bhumibol authorized the recollections of Mr Cléon Séraïdaris to be assembled by his son in this book and published as historic testimony, throwing light on part of the life of our Royal Family during the King's years in Switzerland.

The second part of this work reminds us of the close association and affection between Lausanne, the Canton of Vaud and the Kingdom of Thailand thanks to the personalities who are dedicated to maintaining these cordial relations.

HE Khun Khwankeo Vajarodaya
Grand Chamberlain to His Majesty the King of Thailand
EHL Honorary Professor (Lausanne, Switzerland)

PROLOGUE

Rarely does one have a chance meeting with a monarch. To be then entrusted to teach and guide him in the principles he would form for his life and reign is honour indeed. Such was the exceptional destiny of Cléon Seraïdaris, the author's father, who became personal tutor, from their youth, to HM King Rama VIII and HM King Rama IX. This book is both tribute to Cléon Séraïdaris and testimony to a career that straddled the history of the era.

A few years ago, at a private audience at Klai Kang Wong Palace in Hua Hin, HM King Bhumibol suggested to the author that he undertake this work which would tell the story of the two young Kings and their tutor in Switzerland, stating that these historical facts deserved to be known.

Much has been written of the reign of HM Rama IX. This book, undertaken at the instigation of the King, speaks of events and a period of which the public are largely unaware. Fully supported by fact, it reveals the story of his childhood and that of his elder brother Rama VIII, their family life, their mother Princess Mahidol and their sister Princess Galyani, as well as the role of their tutor, Cléon Séraïdaris. In this, the cordial relations between Thailand and Switzerland will be strengthened with the publication of this book. Symbolic of the friendship of these two nations is that this book was written in celebration of the auspicious occasion of HM King Bhumibol's seventh cycle birthday anniversary in 2011.

L. C. S.

His Majesty King Bhumibol
The photograph has the following handwritten dedication:
To my dear tutor.
P. Mahidol
Lausanne, 29 April 1939

His Majesty King Ananda
The photograph has the following handwritten dedication:
To my dear professor.
From his pupil
Ananda Mahidol
Lausanne, 1 May 1939

Her Royal Highness Princess Sangwal Mahidol

Her Royal Highness Princess Galyani Vadhana

SIMPLIFIED GENEALOGY OF THE ROYAL FAMILY

- HM Queen Saovabha Bhongsri
- Rama V HM Great King Chulalongkorn
- Rama VI HM King Vajiravudh
- Rama VII HM King Prajadhipok
- HRH Princess Galyani Vadhana Krom Luang Naradhiwas Rajanagarindra
- Rama VIII HM King Ananda Mahidol
- HRH Princess Ubol Ratana Raja Kanya
- HRH Crown Prince Maha Vajiralongkorn

```
HM Queen
Sawang Wattana


HRH Prince                    HRH Princess
Mahidol of Songkla            Srinagarindra Mahidol


Rama IX
HM King                       HM Queen Sirikit
Bhumibol Adulyadej


HRH Princess                  HRH Princess
Maha Chakri Sirindhorn        Chulabhorn Walailak
```

FIRST PART
MEMORIES OF THE TUTOR

1

THE FUTURE TUTOR

On 26 July 1906 at the Séraïdaris family home, *Huberstrasse 16*, Dresden (Germany), amidst great joy, Marianthi gave birth to her fifth child, a boy. His father Constantin named him Cléon. The new-born was to join four siblings, all boys, Yannis, his elder by seven years, Nicolaos, Angelos and Pâris. This was a Greek family, engaged in international trade in tobacco, originally hailing from Kavála and most probably from the ancient Grecian community of Alexandria as per the research by Yannis into the family history. Two families, the Séraïdaris and the Zervoudaki, united by marriage, settled in Dresden in 1897 having previously lived in Constantinople, the old name for Istanbul and still a place-name cherished by Greek families.

At the same time, on the other side of the world, Chulalongkorn the Great, His Majesty King Rama V reigned as absolute monarch over the Kingdom of Siam. Constantin and Marianthi could not have imagined that their youngest son, Cléon, would one day be honoured as tutor to the following century's longest-reigning and wise successor to the throne of Siam.

A few years later, Marianthi became seriously ill and in 1916 it was decided that the family would move to Lausanne, Switzerland, to seek treatment for her. The reason for in this move was the presence in Lausanne of Professor César Roux who was practicing there and whose international reputation and fame attracted foreigners who were still able to travel abroad during those war-troubled times. The Séraïdaris family settled in a house named *L'Hiver* at *Avenue Sainte-Luce*.

The parents registered their five sons at a secondary school where they had no difficulty in adapting linguistically; already, when living in Constantinople, the family spoke French at home. In Dresden, the children of course spoke German at school, saving Greek in private. However, their father was intent that the boys should benefit from an intellectually rich and cosmopolitan education. French was at that time the language of diplomats and elite families. Thus, the brothers immediately fitted into this new life as students in an intellectual and already international Lausanne.

Despite receiving the very best of care, Marianthi could not be cured and in 1921 the family preferred to return to Dresden. But Cléon had not yet finished his studies and it was decided that he would remain in Lausanne where he would attend a boarding school, the *École Nouvelle* in Chailly. His parents confided him to the care and surveillance of Christo, his maternal uncle, who was living at *Avenue des Mousquines*. Christo was in the habit of receiving many distinguished friends in his home, Eleftherios Venizélos, President of the Greek Council being one of the most illustrious.

Then in the brutal Wall Street crash of 1929 the Séraïdaris

family lost most of their assets and their material comfort. With the help of his uncle, Cléon did not have to leave his city of adoption but was able to continue his studies there. This was fortunate and his teachers held him to be a talented student and so he proved to be in his law studies at the University of Lausanne. Cléon, in real distinguished young man of his time, occupied his leisure with some fashionable pursuits of the era: tennis, table tennis, football, skiing and motoring.

On 26 November 1930, the Dean of the Faculty of Law at the University of Lausanne conferred a certificate confirming that *"Mr Cléon Séraïdaris has successfully completed the second part of the examinations for his Doctorate in Law and Juridical Sciences"*. All that was now needed was to present and defend his Ph.D. law thesis.

This was indeed a fortunate period in the life of Cléon and to his great happiness he was to meet and marry Magdalena, a delightful young Lausanne lady of Bernese origin, seven years his junior. Such was Magdalena's charm that the famed Swiss artist Rodolphe Théophile Bosshard was inspired to paint her portrait.

Marianthi and Constantin Séraïdaris, Cléon's parents

Pâris, Angelos, Nicolaos, Cléon and Yannis Séraïdaris, around 1911

Cléon cleaning the family's "Benz", August 1925

Greek Council President Elefthérios Venizélos,
Cléon's uncle Christo Zervoudaki and Yannis Séraïdaris on the
terrace of the family house, *Avenue des Mousquines* in Lausanne

Cléon Séraïdaris and his Amilcar automobile in summer 1929 while studying law at the Lausanne University, before meeting the Royal Family

Cléon was a very good tennis player

Yannis, Angelos, Cléon (standing), Nicolaos and Pâris (sitting). All five Séraïdaris brothers were enthusiastic tennis players during their studies in Lausanne

Mr Abrezol, an unidentified friend, Cléon and Mr Landolt

UNIVERSITY OF LAUSANNE
———

The Dean of the Faculty of Law

Lausanne, 26 November 1930

The undersigned, hereby, declares that Mr Cléon Séraïdaris successfully passed the second part of the examinations for his Doctorate in Law and Juridical Sciences last October. To obtain the doctorate degree he simply has to present and defend his thesis.

This statement is not a diploma.

The Dean of the Faculty of Law,

Eugène Cordey

Translation of the document of the right page

UNIVERSITÉ DE LAUSANNE

LE DOYEN
DE LA
FACULTÉ DE DROIT

Lausanne, le 26 novembre 1930.

Le soussigné déclare que Monsieur Cléon Sérardaris a subi avec succès la seconde partie des examens du doctorat en droit, mention sciences juridiques, au mois d'octobre dernier, et que pour obtenir le grade de docteur en droit, il n'a plus qu'à présenter et à soutenir la dissertation et les thèses accessoires réglementaires.

La présente déclaration ne constitue pas un diplôme.

Le doyen de la Faculté de droit   Eug. Courcey

Statement of the Dean of Lausanne Faculty of Law

Portrait of Magdalena by Rodolphe Théophile Bosshard

Portrait of Magdalena and Cléon by photographer Nelly's
(Elli Séraïdaris, Angelos's wife, one of Cléon's brothers)

2

HISTORIC ENCOUNTER

During the period that followed, Cléon started to write his thesis. He could not ignore the fact that the family's financial difficulties required him to find a job to provide a better life, especially as Magdalena and he had now their first son, Léandre, elder brother of the author. So, to his great credit, Cléon taught tennis and, like many another impecunious students, also taught after-school class for pupils needing extra coaching.

Cléon and Magdalena had formed a close friendship with Rasmi Suriyong, a Siamese Prince, descendant of King Rama IV. Rasmi, studying medicine in Lausanne, had married a Lausanne young girl called Marcelle. Rasmi, being of an insightful and sensitive intellect, immediately grasped the charisma and erudition of his friend Cléon and it was this understanding that resulted in the changing of Cléon's future.

It came about thus that Prince Mahidol of Songkla, third son of King Rama V had studied medicine and, in order to complete his training, his studies took him abroad from Siam accompanied by his young wife, Princess Sangwal Mahidol, whom he had met while she was studying nursing, achieving distinction as head of her class. Their first daughter, Princess Galyani, was born in London in 1923, followed by their first son, Prince Ananda in 1925 at Heidelberg, Germany, and then in 1927 by Prince Bhumibol, in Cambridge, United States. When Prince Mahidol of Songkla and his family returned home to Siam, his health deteriorated and, in the prime of his life, he passed away in 1929.

In 1932, King Rama VII abdicated. Several months later, in 1933, Princess Mahidol took her three children to Switzerland where the climate was particularly favourable to the health of the young Prince Ananda who would soon become King Rama VIII and with the intention that they receive their education in its famed schools. Switzerland's tradition of neutrality provided guaranteed stability for the family, unlike the situation across Europe at that time as history will prove unfortunately a few years later. The Royal Family came to settle in Lausanne, the city where the Mahidol family had already made a short and pleasant stay in 1928. The Princess loved the charm of this student city and decided to settle there temporarily into an elegant apartment at *Avenue Tissot 16*. Children began their schooling at the *Miremont* School where they learned the basics of the French language.

In 1936, Rasmi Suriyong, knowing the fine qualities of his friend Cléon, now moved to recommend him to Princess Mahidol, as personal tutor to her sons, Ananda and Bhumibol. The empathy between the Royal Family and Cléon was clear and the Princess Mother asked him to tutor the young King and Prince. Cléon was deeply honoured and indeed touched and without hesitation accepted this most prestigious post to which he thereafter dedicated himself.

Prince Mahidol of Songkla in London, 1923

Princess Mahidol and her three children
during a short stay in Lausanne, October 1928

3

VADHANA VILLA

For the Royal children, the first months of their new life in Lausanne were very different from that in Sra Pathum Palace, the residence of the Mahidol family where they had lived before leaving Bangkok. Cléon was a true guide for this very united family, far from their country during the time the studies would last. One of the first decisions of Princess Mahidol was to search for a calm and secluded residence suitable for her family, staff and visitors.

In Pully, east of Lausanne, a large villa was found at *Chemin de Chamblandes 51*, which, when they took up residence, Princess Mahidol chose to name "Vadhana". Nearby was the home of General Henri Guisan, famed Commander in Chief of the Swiss Army during the 1939–45 war.

At Vadhana Villa Princess Mahidol determined that she would personally nurture Bee, Nant and Lek (these were her children's intimate names at home for Galyani, Ananda and Bhumibol). Cléon was to assist, taking charge of the educational development such that a King should receive. With his experience of the demanding curriculum of *École Nouvelle* in Chailly, he was able to recommend that his young charges be enrolled there. Princess Mahidol agreed and the stage was set for a successful education for her sons. Princess Mahidol had a precise vision that the children's education should reflect the unique and responsible duties they would need to equip them to be good and wise in the posts that would fall to them, as assigned by their birth. Cléon shared this vision and set about fulfilling the mission which the Princess Mother had entrusted to him. His career with the Thai Royal Family for the next twenty-six years had commenced.

Cléon lived with his family in an apartment only a mile from the royal residence which allowed him to be conveniently on duty there to perform his tasks. He realized that while his charges were King and Prince, Ananda and Bhumibol were also children. Children who required constant attention, encouragement and the naturally caring presence of the Princess Mother. For Princess Mahidol her children were a fond reminder of her husband and her understanding that they would be called upon to personify the future of the Kingdom.

Cléon's duties were especially gratifying as both his charges were bright in their studies and, despite their youth, behaved responsibly beyond their age. They were conscientious students, while fully aware of the often heavy future responsibility of Kingdom and leadership inescapably assigned to them. Both boys, King and Prince, had shared talents, unaware that fate's hand would write for each a different history.

Outside school, King and Prince were encouraged into

sports: cycling, tennis, table tennis, ice-skating... A well-known Lausanne lawyer, Mr Philippe Jaques, a King's contemporary at *École Nouvelle*, remembers that Ananda was invincible at table tennis and difficult to keep pace with at cycling. In winter, the entire family, staying in the mountains, took pleasure in skiing.

Other skills and recreations for Ananda and Bhumibol were wide-ranging, from mycology to gardening, auto-mechanics and, like all boys of their ages games such as chess, scale model cars and trains. It was at this time that the two boys with their sister founded the Patapoum Club, a fictitious association of imaginary characters, whose roles were played out by the children. This "Club" allowed an outlet for the sorts of harmless mischief that enabled them to look inward and develop in play. Though destined for a studious future, their need for enjoyment and sheer fun was as important as it was for other children with a lighter destiny.

When not busy with his charges, Cléon was much appreciated by the Siamese entourage of the Royal Family for his excellence as a bridge partner, the fashionable game of an evening in the 1930s.

Vadhana Villa in winter

January 1938

Cléon photographed by the King at Vadhana Villa

King Ananda taking care of his vegetable garden

Princess Mahidol loved to take care of her flowers

King Ananda and Prince Bhumibol at Vadhana Villa

King Ananda in class at the *École Nouvelle*

The two future Kings in the schoolyard

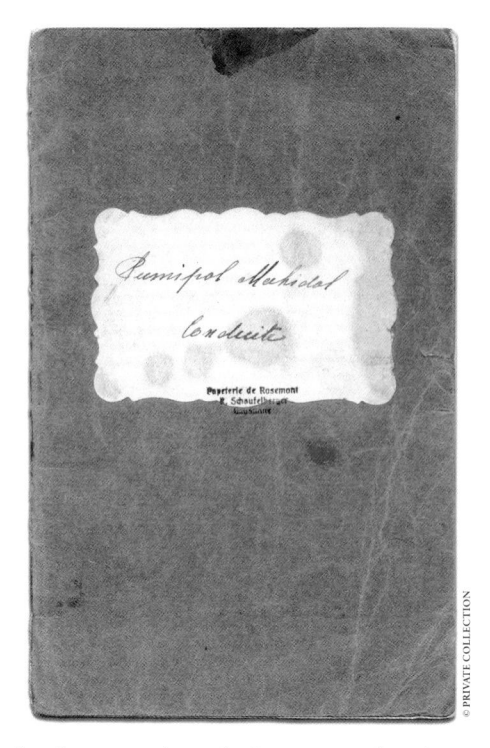

School record book of Prince Bhumibol, very good and very devoted student

The Princess Mother and her two sons in Vadhana Villa's garden

The Princess Mother and her three children in Vadhana Villa's garden

The Royal Family in Vadhana Villa's garden in March 1939

Princess Galyani and her brothers at Vadhana Villa

4

LIFE AT HOME

The Royal Family went to the mountains regularly; in Valais at Champex, in the Bernese Alps at Adelboden and Petite Scheidegg, in the Bernese Oberland at Saanenmöser, or in the Canton of Vaud, at Villars-sur-Ollon and Arveyes. By the end of the 1930s they preferred the Grisons, Arosa and Davos as the vacation places they valued most, especially for the end of year celebrations. These vacations favoured the young King Ananda's health and allowed the family to develop friendly relations in a relaxed atmosphere.

It was in Lausanne that King Bhumibol found his passion for music, first as player, then as player-composer. Some compositions, such as "Blue Night", achieved Broadway review fame (1951). Many became popular in Thailand where they are very often broadcast.

As a great lover of jazz, the King will play several instruments: piano, clarinet, saxophone, drums… Many years after, at the age of more than fifty, he learned to play the trumpet. As an anecdote, on King Bhumibol's fifth cycle birthday anniversary*, Cléon went to Bangkok to present his good wishes and was both surprised and delighted when the King demonstrated his mastery of the trumpet.

During the summer of 1938, the King and Prince were sent to a summer camp at Zimmerli Institute at Adelboden, along with their tutor. Throughout the stay, the director of the establishment kept incognito the identity of his two distinguished guest, according to the wishes of the Royal Family.

At the same time Princess Mahidol took vacation and rest on the Ligurian Coast of Italy and on the French Riviera at Antibes. The Princess wrote to Cléon almost every day asking for news of her sons whom she called affectionately her *bambini* as one can see on a postcard sent from Genoa. Cléon was asked to send his letters to her at the next stopping places to ensure that she receive them swiftly as there were not many telephone connections at that time.

On 2 August 1938, the Princess sent a postcard from Antibes with a picture of a water-skier on it. She wrote that she did not have the courage to try it and that she thought it was not as nice as skiing on snow.

---

*In Thai culture, the important birthdays are celebrated by cycles of twelve years. The most important of these starts with the fifth cycle, or at sixty years of age.

HM King Ananda, Champex, 1936

King Ananda and Prince Bhumibol, Champex, 1936

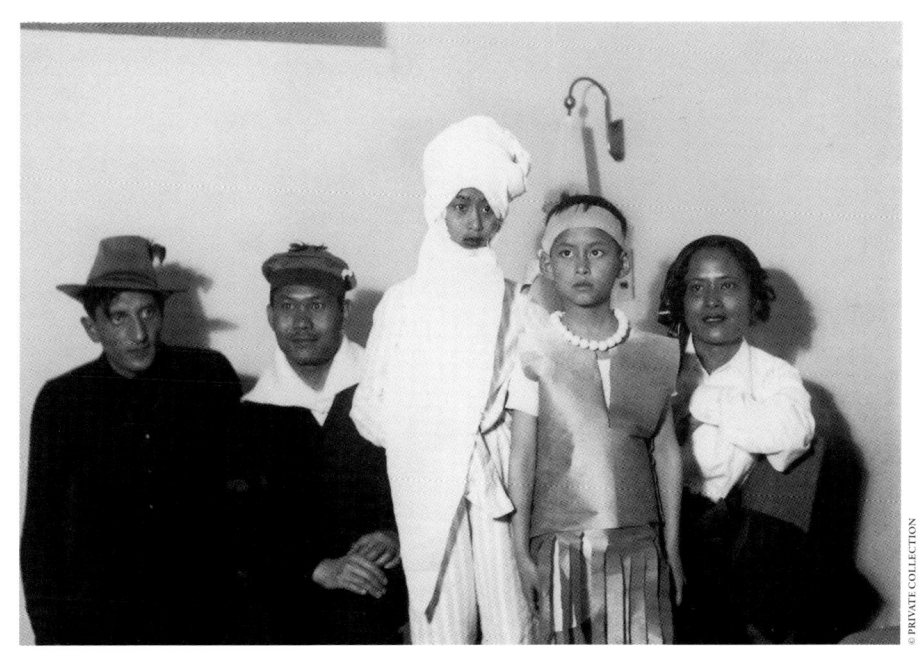

Costume party at Arosa, 31 December 1936

King Ananda and the tutor, Arosa, 1937

The two Kings with Princess Mahidol and Cléon, Arosa, 1937

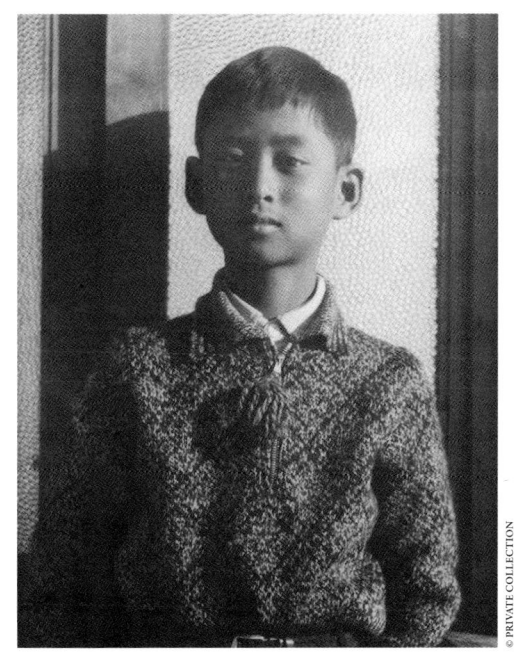

King Ananda at Arosa in January 1937

Champex, 1937

The two Kings with Cléon at Champex in 1937

Adelboden, summer 1938

Adelboden, summer 1938

King Rama VIII during his stay at Adelboden

Adelboden, summer 1938,
the two Kings with their tutor

Postcard from Antibes

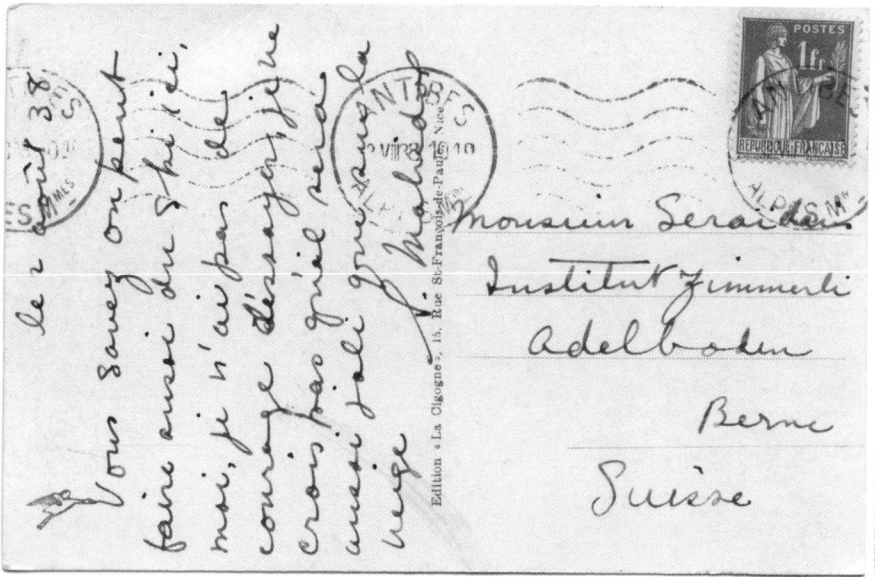

Postcard from Portofino

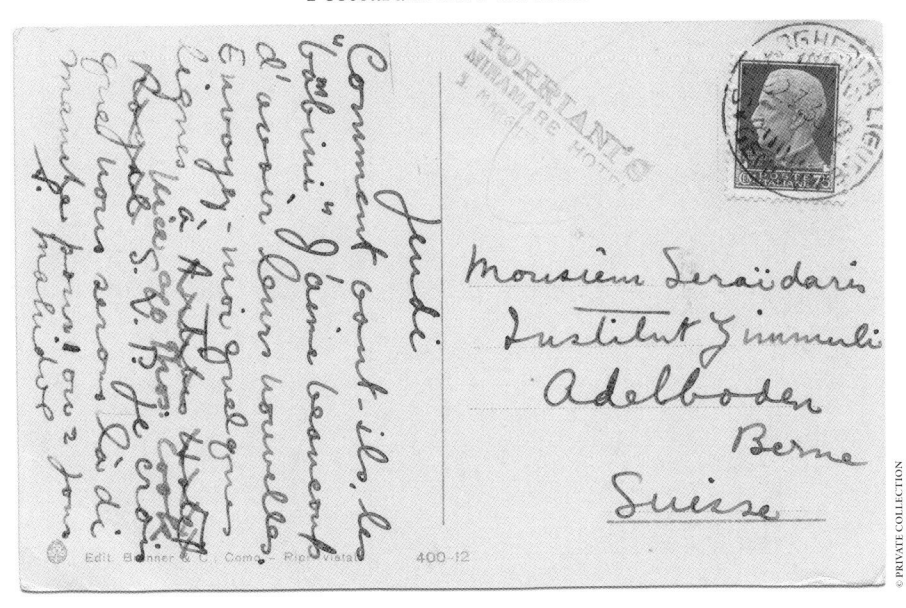

Princess Mahidol at a New Year's Eve party in 1938 along with Cléon,
Prince Vichitwongwuthikrai, Ambassador of Thailand in Bern, and Lady Sae

© PRIVATE COLLECTION

Arosa, 1938: Prince Bhumibol, Cléon, King Ananda and
Ms Sawate Chanruan, lady-in-waiting of Princess Mahidol

Cléon and King Ananda

The Princess Mother and Prince Bhumibol

January 1938

Arosa, January 1938
The two Kings are playing ice hockey with Cléon

King Ananda and the Princess Mother at the skating rink, Arosa, March 1939

Princess Mahidol skiing, Arosa, January 1938

90

An igloo construction at Arosa

King Ananda and Prince Bhumibol are skating,
following their tutor's advice at Arosa, March 1939

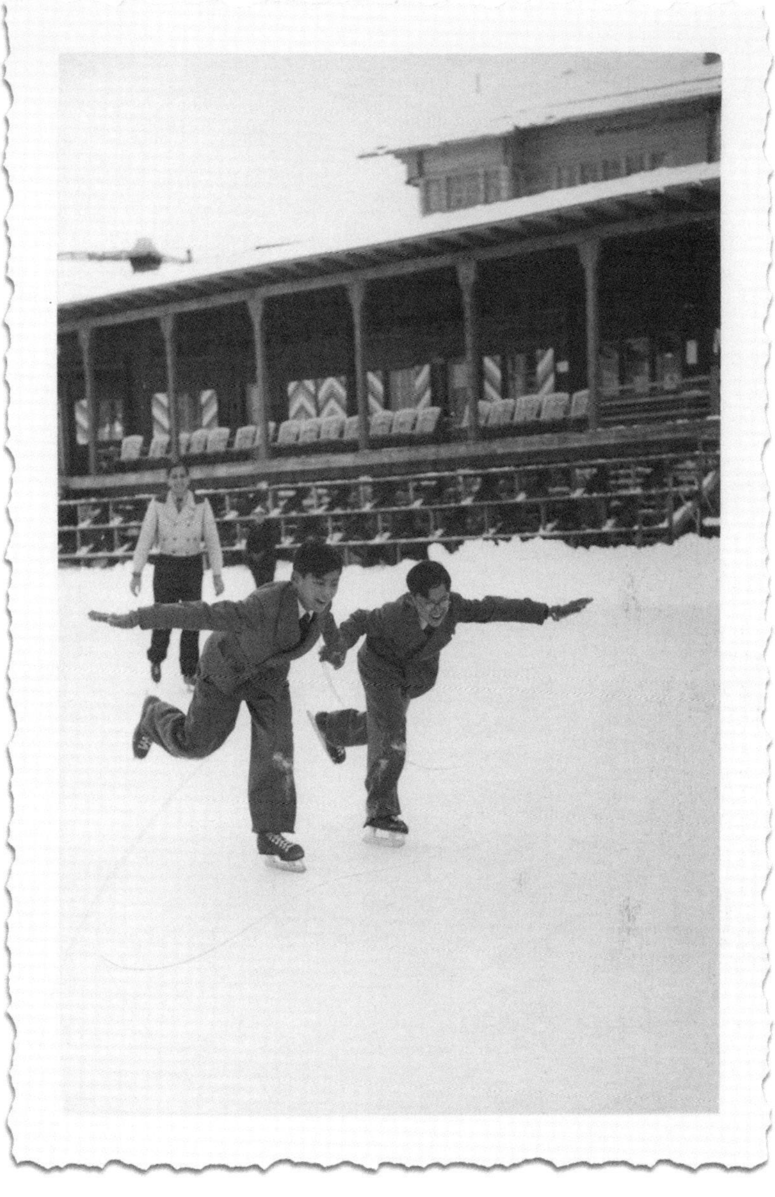

Arosa, 1939

The Royal Family just before leaving with Cléon driving the
Mercedes-Benz Nürburg, Arosa, March 1939

5

TEMPORARY RETURN TO THE KINGDOM

In September 1938, the Royal Family announced that they would be returning to Bangkok for a few months. Cléon could now go back to writing his Ph.D. law thesis. In the event that the Royal Family may need to stay in Thailand and not return to Lausanne, Princess Mahidol instructed her private secretary, Khun Anek Satrabhaya, to write an end of employment reference for Cléon, giving him a glowing recommendation as tutor. The Princess also entrusted her cat, Tito, to Cléon. The Vadhana Villa was however kept as the Princess Mother intended that they should return.

A mutual rapport had grown between Nant, Lek and Cléon. This was based on respect and liking of one another. Cléon reflected on the commitment the boys gave to their studies and the Princess Mother found Cléon to be entirely trustworthy and devoted to her sons' advancement in education and character. Therefore the departure was difficult for them all and, although return was anticipated, indeed intended, nothing could be guaranteed.

A farewell dinner was held on 10 October 1938, then came the morning of departure. There was a wistfulness, a sense of regret as the Royal Family departed from Lausanne at the start of a long sea journey. Thankfully, there were letters and postcards from each of the ship's stopovers telling Cléon about the voyage, anecdotes, etc. These served to reassure him as it was a radical change to their daily life. King Ananda had recently celebrated his thirteenth birthday and Prince Bhumibol was about to celebrate his eleventh on arrival in Bangkok.

※ ※ ※

Letters at sea

The Royal Family expressed themselves remarkably well in French. The re-transcribed letters hereafter reflect exactly the informal atmosphere and the intimacy that existed between the Royal Family and the tutor.

18 October 1938
The family wrote a number of postcards from Marseille before sailing on the Danish ship *M/S Meonia*:

We arrived this morning in Marseille and we are leaving the harbour at noon. I hope everybody is well over there. Our rooms are comfortable. We do not have time to eat "bouillabaisse". Signed: *Ananda Mahidol.*

Another reads: *One eats well in the morning.* Signed: *Pumipol Mahidol.* Then the Princess Mother added: *Thank you for the beautiful flowers.* Signed: *S. Mahidol.*

The letters at this period are still quite formal, while they would become more familiar in the future, as evens unfolded.

23 October 1938

This date was favourable for the whole family to write: a letter in the morning, then a postcard early afternoon and finally a long letter in the evening. The morning letter and the postcard were posted on board the *Meonia* at Port Said. The first letter, handwritten by Ananda, started as follow:

Dear Sir, we have the pleasure of announcing to you that we have all arrived safe and sound at Port Said. After having crossed the Strait of Bonifacio, the sea was very calm. On Thursday, we passed the Stromboli volcano which was still active. One could see the flame and a piece of a broken crater. Then the Strait of Messina (8 a.m.). On Friday, we gave our birthday message to Madame*. Then in the evening we passed Crete, without seeing it. On Saturday the sea was very rough and today at this very moment the pilot has come up to guide the boat into the harbour. In the meantime we play deck-tennis, deck-golf and table tennis.

Then followed a sentence in English (as the Royal Family wrote all correspondence in French): *Mrs Vigit has seasickness*, meaning the wife of the Thai Ambassador posted in Bern.

Still in the same letter, a message from their mother: *It is now ten o'clock in the morning and we arrive at Port Said. The boat sails slowly into the harbour. It is going to stop in a few minutes' time, I think. I am going to get ready to go into town. Goodbye.*
Signed: *S.*
Then handwritten by Nant: *Respectfully yours, sir.*
Signed: *Ananda Mahidol* and *P. Mahidol.*

---

* Author's note: "Madame" is the usual name the children and Cléon would call Princess Mahidol at Lausanne.

Underneath, one could read in recognizable, nice handwriting in spite of her tender age: *Best wishes.*
Signed: *Galyani.*
P.S. We have just received your letter, added Ananda.

*

The afternoon postcard, handwritten by Ananda also posted on board the *Meonia* in Port Said, says:
We will pass the Suez Canal this evening. This morning we visited the city. We bought pith helmets, a magnifying glass, handcuffs, revolvers, etc. The sentence continues in the hand of the Princess Mother: *and a large hat, soap, etc.*
Signed: *S. Mahidol* and *A. Mahidol.*

*

The third letter, the beginning of which was also written on 23 October at Port Said, was finished in the evening at sea and sent by the *Meonia* post office during the stopover at Aden as evidenced by stamps. This letter written only by Princess Mahidol stands as an historical documentation describing the simplicity of the family's life, especially that of the two Kings. Here it is, in its entirety:

Suez Canal, 23 October
Dear Sir, your letters made us very happy. I am starting to feel nostalgic for Lausanne and I feel so far from it whereas your letter brings me closer a little to it.

Thank you for your best wishes on my birthday. The children's letter is very nice.

I do not know how the captain knew it was my birthday, he invited me up on the bridge at 11.30 a.m. for champagne and he gave me a Copenhagen porcelain ashtray, it is really kind!

We feel very much "at home" on this boat. The captain is very kind. He eats at our table. I am next to him, and so I learn a lot of things from him. The children have already told you what sports we play: deck-tennis, deck-golf and table tennis, but yesterday we could not do much because the sea was quite rough and many people fell ill, Nant and Lek were also a little sick.

Suez Gulf, 23 October

At Port Said, we did a lot of shopping. There were nice things in leather. It was rather hot in the shop. After shopping, we came back on the boat for lunch. The Danish lunch is not like other lunches, first they give us a hot dish, then everyone goes to look for what they want at the tables placed in the middle of the dining room, where there are a lot of good things, cold meat, salads, lobster, prawns, bear ham, fish, "pickles", etc. If one does not have enough at the first serving, one can start anew. After that, cheese or fruit.

They have installed a swimming pool this morning, it is 3½ by 2½ metres, you can imagine that we cannot do much in there, but we were able to enjoy ourselves quite a lot this afternoon.

They have just told us that we are near Sinai.

Red Sea, 26 October

It has been so hot these last two days, it is 33 degrees in my cabin at the moment, 11.15 p.m. (10 p.m. in Lausanne). One dance on the deck with the gramophone, my cabin is on this deck and I can hear it quite well. The children, especially Lek, are a bit tired in this heat.

We have started to work since the 20th and it is going quite well, myself I am not doing much, I am reading three books: "Catherine", "Mer Rouge" and "La passion de Yong Kwei Fui". I find Catherine interesting, her character, her ability and her numerous lovers.

This afternoon, we passed the Islands of the 12 Apostles. These islands are completely bare; on the biggest island, there is a lighthouse with the keeper's house, this house is the only thing, there is nothing at all apart from this. The poor keeper lives there with his family for six months and then he has two months holiday to go back home. It seems that almost all the lighthouse keepers at the Red Sea are of Greek nationality. Greeks must love living in isolation!

It is less hot today, and the sea is a little rough.

Aden 28 October
We arrive here at 2.15 p.m. I hope everyone is well. The children send you their fond regards.
Signed: *S. Mahidol*.

*

16 November 1938
A postcard picturing King Rama I bridge sent from Bangkok informs the tutor of the family's safe arrival. It

was signed by P. Mahidol and A. Mahidol mentioning: *"We passed under this bridge in a warship yesterday".*

*

27 November 1938

This letter gave more detailed news, this time signed by the Patapoum Club. It started without formality, saying:

We have received your numerous letters and thank you very much. We have a nice room with a desk, and on this desk there are two "Eversharp" pens, one of them is adjustable, they work very well, should they be taken back to Lausanne?

Over here, something new happened during the voyage, the Club has taken possession of 32 shillings and during our stay in Bangkok we have 160 bahts! Approximately 280 francs!

We have also received 2 two-seater electric cars, all red. Up until today we have been on strike since Penang! And tomorrow lessons will begin. In the garden, there are little snakes coming out at night whose bite is fatal, of course if one has injections and other things, one does not die. We have seen two of them. There is one in the garden pond and we go boating and play fireworks.

We are not suffering from heat but from mosquitoes. Here is a specimen killed by the Monkey ("the Monkey" is a member responsible for propaganda, according to the "official statutes" of the Patapoum Club!).

Now the big ceremonies have finished and the school????? Ah! Hem!???

Signed: *The entire Patapoum Club sends you ~ ~ ~* (voluntarily illegible signs).

Inside, there still is seventy-five years after this letter was written, a mosquito squashed between two pages, with a warning in red ink and in capital letters: *BE CAREFUL INSIDE THERE IS AN ANIMAL. DO NOT LET IT FALL.* This letter to their tutor handwritten by Ananda, but from both Kings, was touching.

*

5 December 1938

Lek's eleventh birthday, no mention of celebrations, but the Princess wrote from Bangkok a thank you letter to Cléon for his last letter, and sent her best wishes to him and his family.

*

The next day, on the other hand, the children wrote to their tutor:

6 December

We are going to tell you about the things that we are doing and what is happening over here. Everyday except Sunday we start by working a little bit.

Then we enjoy ourselves playing with the electric cars and go boating.

In the afternoon we take a rest, we take tea and almost everyday there is a ceremony. But one day Miss Hersch wanted to go sailing. There were three boats, a big one, a middle-sized one and a tiny one that was rather difficult to sail. And it was in the small one that she wanted to go because she had seen Mrs Vichit go in it. She went on board, and she had hardly gone 1 metre when she sunk. Her dress was all wet. The "mom" gave her clothes and she could leave, but she wanted to try sailing again only in a bathing costume.

Meanwhile we have received a grain of rice with an inscription of 378 letters, an electric boat with a battery and we run it with electricity.

At the celebration of the Monkey, the house was full of presents.

Signed: *The Patapoum Club sends you ~ ~ ~* (voluntarily illegible signs).

Pictures cut from the *Popeye Journal* were attached, very much the trend in Europe at that time, but certainly not in French in Bangkok! (Later the Royal children also became assiduous readers of Tintin adventures.)

*

17 December 1938

Ananda wrote to Cléon to thank him for having sent some handkerchiefs which he liked very much. He also told him that he and his brother had received as toys two aeroplanes with petrol engine that did not yet work very well and that they also had an extra engine, mounted separately on a wooden stand.

Also received was a train each wagon being approximately 1.50 to 2 metres long. There were 20 wagons with windows and folding tables inside. All built to scale. There was even a steam locomotive that worked by compressed air, which they could sit both inside or on top.

Today we went swimming and everybody knows how to swim.

In ending Ananda added that recently the Government had issued a new 1 baht banknote, he attached both an old banknote and a sample of the new one.

This letter is signed: *Patapoum Club.*

*

1 January
Patapoum Club, Bangkok.
We were able to make one of the power-driven planes fly. It turned in a circle and it fell and broke the wing. It was repaired with the glider's wood, as we feel too lazy to do it, there are so many nice things. It has been rebuilt, but is a little damaged by the fall. We have received two small boats with an aeroplane engine. They sail very fast. Each time we make them run, the whole body goes back up on the ground. We hope to be able to make them sail on the lake with our electric boat, because electric boats with an aeroplane engine are rather fragile. We are sending you 2 samples of a four-leaved clover, because there are so many of them. Miss Hersch is sick, our lessons have also lessened. We are always quite busy with the ceremonies. Greetings from the Patapoum Club.

PS: We are collecting coins and we asked someone for old coins, and a few days later, everybody brought them.

Tito, the two Kings' faithful companion during their childhood

Khun Anek Satrabhaya, Princess Mahidol's private Secretary

- Vadhana -
Chamblandes-dessus

I, the undersigned, hereby certify that Mr C. Séraïdaris has been engaged during the past two years as a tutor to the two children of Mrs Mahidol.

I am authorized to say that Mr Séraïdaris has fulfilled his function in a brilliant way. He indeed has all the qualities required to carry out his task: awareness, patience, tact and knowledge, etc. His excellent knowledge of child psychology allowed him to earn the trust and confidence of the two children who viewed him more as a good friend than a strict and boring teacher.

Since Mrs Mahidol and her family are expected to return to their country, they are forced to relinquish with regret the dedicated and loyal service of Mr Séraïdaris. Mrs Mahidol heartily recommends Mr Séraïdaris to those parents who are seeking a good tutor for their children.

A. Satrabhaya
Secretary

Lausanne, 8 October 1938

Vadhana
Chamblandes-dessus

    Je, soussigné, certifie que monsieur C. Seraidaris fut engagé, durant deux années, comme précepteur des deux enfants de madame Mahidol.

    Je suis autorisé à dire que monsieur Seraidaris s'est accquitté de sa fonction d'une façon fort brillante. Il possède en effet toutes les qualités requises pour mener à bien sa tâche: conscience, patience, tact et savoir, etc... Connaissant admirablement la psychologie des enfants, c'est ce qui le rend, aux yeux de ceux-ci, non comme un maître sévère et ennuyeux, mais plutôt un bon camerade digne de toutes les sympathies et à qui ils accordent spontanément leur confiance.

    Madame Mahidol et sa famille, devant rentrer dans leur pays, se voient obliger de renoncer avec regret aux bons services de monsieur Seraidaris et le recommandent chaleureusement à ceux qui voudraient trouver un bon précepteur pour leurs enfants.

A. Sabrabhaga

le secrétaire.

Fait à Lausanne, ce 8 octobre 1938.

The tutor's work certificate requested by Princess Mahidol in case the Royal Family could not return to Switzerland in January 1939
(See translation on the left page)

Postcard dated 18 October 1938

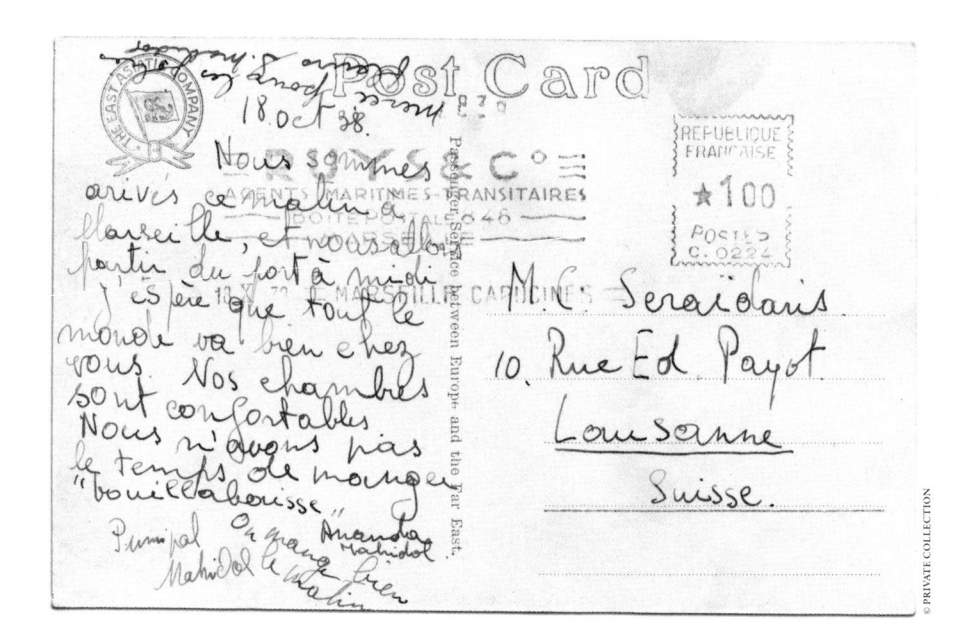

Postcard dated 16 November 1938, King Rama I Bridge

16 novembre 38
Nous avons passé
sous ce pont dans
un navire de
guerre hier.

L. Mahidol   P. Mahidol

M. Cléon Se...aris
10. Rue Ed. Payot
Lausanne
(Suisse)

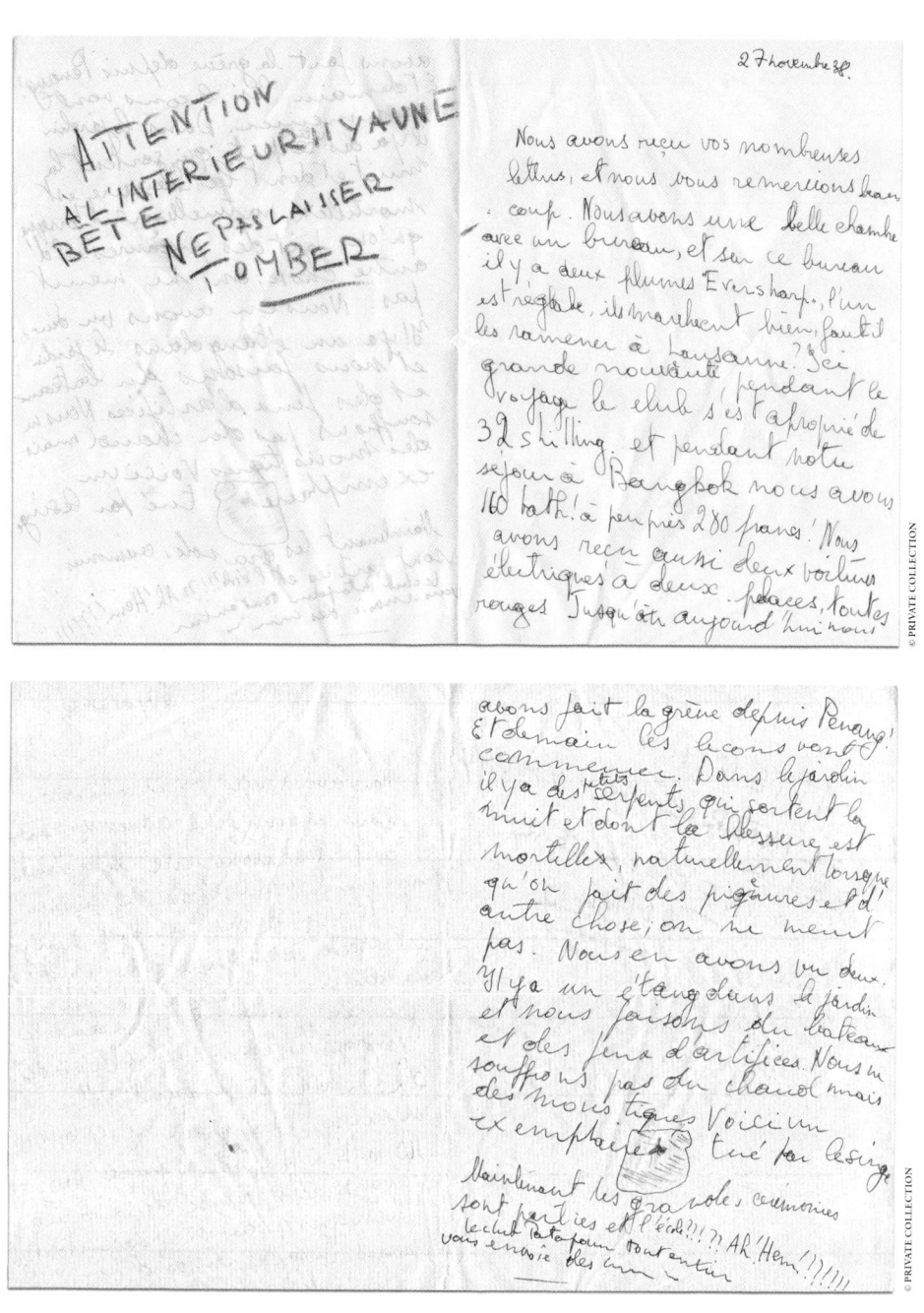

The mosquito's letter dated 27 November, with its envelope

The young Kings pilot a sailing boat scale model

Christmas wishes 1938 signed by the Patapoum Club

116

With Kindest Thoughts
and
Best Wishes for Christmas
and the New Year.

Chula Pakaporn

First series of 1 baht banknotes bearing the image of King Rama VIII

6

RETURN TO STUDIOUS LIFE IN SWITZERLAND

A few months later, by the beginning of 1939, the Royal Family had returned to Lausanne and immediately restarted their daily life with Cléon who had enjoyed the few months "vacation".

During the consideration regarding the two young men's studies, His Majesty King Ananda was inclined toward the law as this was the logical path for him as King whose responsibilities would be over Thai law, while Prince Bhumibol will chose science studies for which he always had a predilection. If fate had not decided otherwise, King Rama VIII would have reigned and developed the laws of his country and his brother would have assisted him in advancing the scientific areas of the Kingdom.

In fact, it was this choice of a science-based education that would later enable King Rama IX, on top of his constitutional tasks, to perform and oversee the great scientific and technical works of the Kingdom thanks to his first studies at Lausanne, before choosing at the time of his accession to the throne the Faculty of Law. With continuous support from his tutor, himself a lawyer, that became easily possible.

While the war that darkened the European sky and the implication of Japan in the Asian turmoil engaged the keen mind of the young sovereign Ananda, these matters did not yet disturb the daily routine of the Royal Family at Lausanne.

As it proved, Princess Mahidol's decision to settle the family in Switzerland was wise. Had they resided in another European country they would have probably been obliged to remove to the United States or Australia. Neither was the return to Thailand without its tensions and risks. Such a move would likely have changed the boys' educational focus to English and away from French-speaking orientation.

The Princess Mother firmly objected to departing from Switzerland, which had no justification in her eyes.

The daily life at Vadhana Villa had therefore not changed, in spite of international tensions, including those in Thailand. The Thai Government, given that King Ananda was a young adolescent, sought to have him return to Thailand to ensure his safety. The Princess Mother flatly refused. Her judgement was that the situation in Switzerland was neither critical nor unsafe. Once more Princess Mahidol displayed clear-sightedness.

Of course security measures were taken by the Swiss authorities. In case the situation in the country really put the Royal Family in danger, they had in place a solid plan involving an escape route through France, Spain and Portugal. From there the family could have boarded a liner leaving for the United States. In the garage at Vadhana Villa one limousine was kept ready at all times to leave Pully quickly if the Swiss authorities thought it necessary. Fortunately the need did not arise.

The studies set by Cléon at the Vadhana Villa continued uninterrupted. To these were added sporting activities, excursions and latterly the Royal children were introduced by Cléon to cabinet-making. Cléon had learnt this discipline at the *École Nouvelle* and later became proficient for this art as he had the benefit being tutored by his father-in-law, a professional cabinet-maker who taught him the subtleties and secrets of this, the high art of woodworking, known only to the elite elderly craftsmen.

A near-professional workshop was established at Vadhana Villa. Soon, with great skill, both King and Prince were enthusiastic, such as they were able to craft a variety of fine objects. Prince Bhumibol excelled in making small pieces of furniture and particularly superb model aeroplanes and Thai warships.

Leisure was not neglected. There were bicycles with a Cucciolo motor. This was a great novelty at that time (the commercial Mobylette was not yet available). Folding motorcycles were also supplied from the United States Army Parachutists. King Bhumibol was especially interested in all kind of technological devices and inventions and Cléon was delighted to share with him the discovery of many *avant-garde* inventions from the leading innovators of the era.

From his young age, Prince Bhumibol's main passions were photography and music. He made an assiduous study of both disciplines, comparable to professionals. He set up his own photo-developing laboratory and during long journeys by sea would develop and print films himself on board ship. As an anecdote, while on voyage on the *M/S Selandia*, he wrote to Cléon that he had to use ice to cool the developing trays because the temperature in his cabin was too hot.

Photography had an important role afterwards as he was able to take photographs when out in the field to illustrate the reports and instructions he gave to his General Staff.

The tutor teaches cabinet-making to King Ananda

Model of a ship of the Royal Thai Marine made by HM King Bhumibol

Zurich, 19 August 1939

Vadhana Villa, 23 September 1939

December 1939

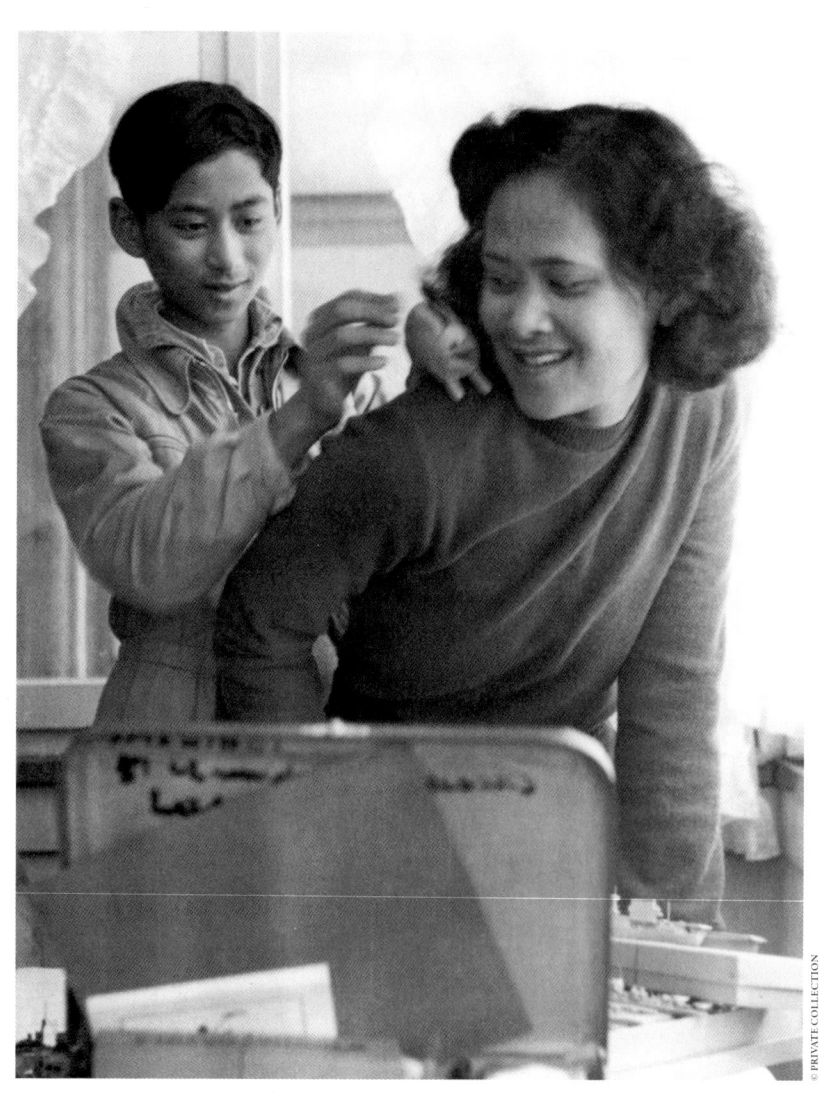

Arosa, January 1940

Summer camp at *La Clairière*, Arveyes, 1940

The two Kings and Cléon ready for a bicycle ride
at *La Clairière*, Arveyes, summer 1940

Summer camp at *La Clairière*, Arveyes, 1940

King Bhumibol and the football team
at *La Clairière*, Arveyes, summer 1940

La Clairière, Arveyes

We spent a really wonderful day. We received many beautiful flowers and the welcome at the chalet was absolutely charming.

    Sangwan Mahidol

      Ananda

        Pumipol

And I ate so well !

           Galyani

Bharadi

Pensri   *All the best*

                                       Cléon Séraïdaris

      24 July 1940

Translation of the document of the right page

> C'est une vraiment magnifique journée que nous avons passée. Nous avons eu beaucoup de belles fleurs et l'accueil au Chalet était tout à fait charmant.
>
> Sangwan Mahidol
> Chenobra
> Punipol
>
> Et ce que j'ai bien mangé !
>
> Galya
>
> Bhanadi
> Pensri
>
> Bien amicalement
> Chindecatanis
>
> 24-VII.40.

Visitors Book, *La Clairière*, Arveyes

King Ananda in 1940

King Ananda at a tennis match, summer 1941

Princess Mahidol and Princess Galyani celebrate the New Year 1941 in Davos with Prince Vichitwongwuthikrai, Lady Sae and Cléon

The Princess Mother and the tutor at winter sports, Davos, 1942

Davos, Weissfluhjoch, Easter 1942.
King Ananda and Cléon with two children from the village

Davos, 1942. Princess Mahidol with one of the photographer's colleagues dressed up as a polar bear

During winter holidays, Prince Bhumibol continued studying piano

Arosa, 1 January 1944, King Ananda's last New Year's Eve in Switzerland, with Princess Mahidol and Cléon, along with Princess Galyani and her husband, Khun Aram Ratanakul and, on the left, Prince Chula Chakrabongse

Davos, 1944. A friend of the family, Princess Mahidol, Prince Bhumibol, Khun Aram Ratanakul, King Ananda, Princess Galyani. In the background Cléon and a close friend

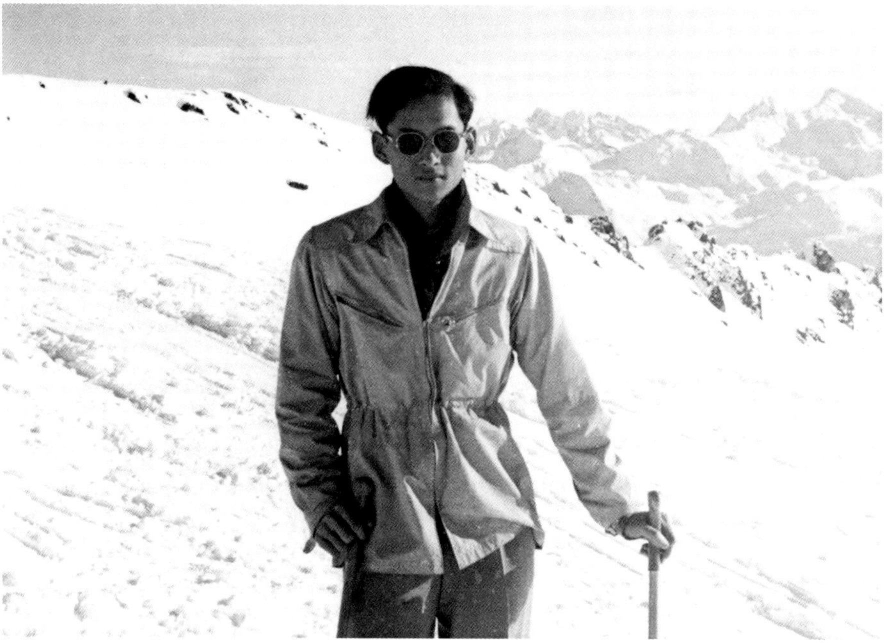

© PRIVATE COLLECTION

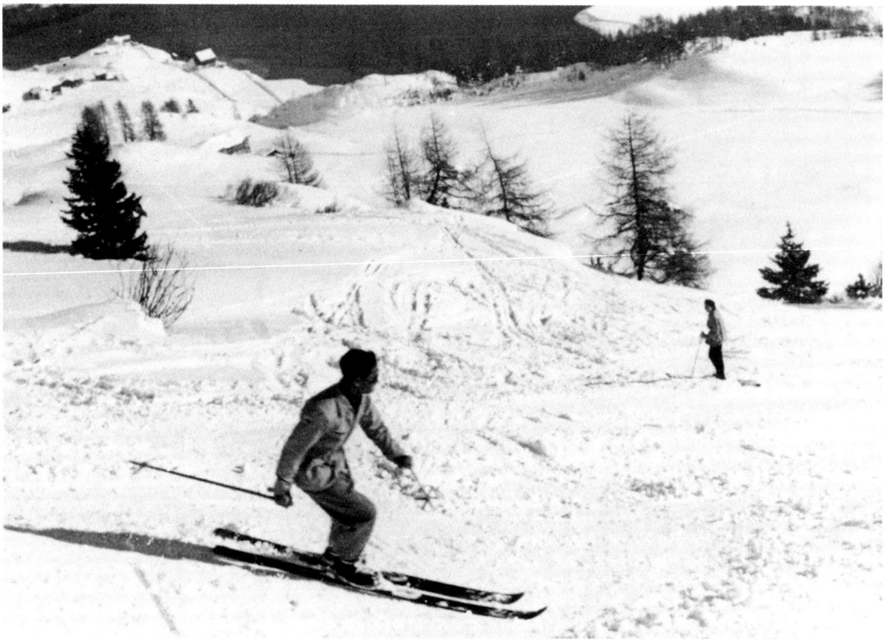

© PRIVATE COLLECTION

King Ananda, Alpe des Chaux, 1944

Princess Galyani, January 1944

Princess Mahidol photographing her family

HM King Ananda

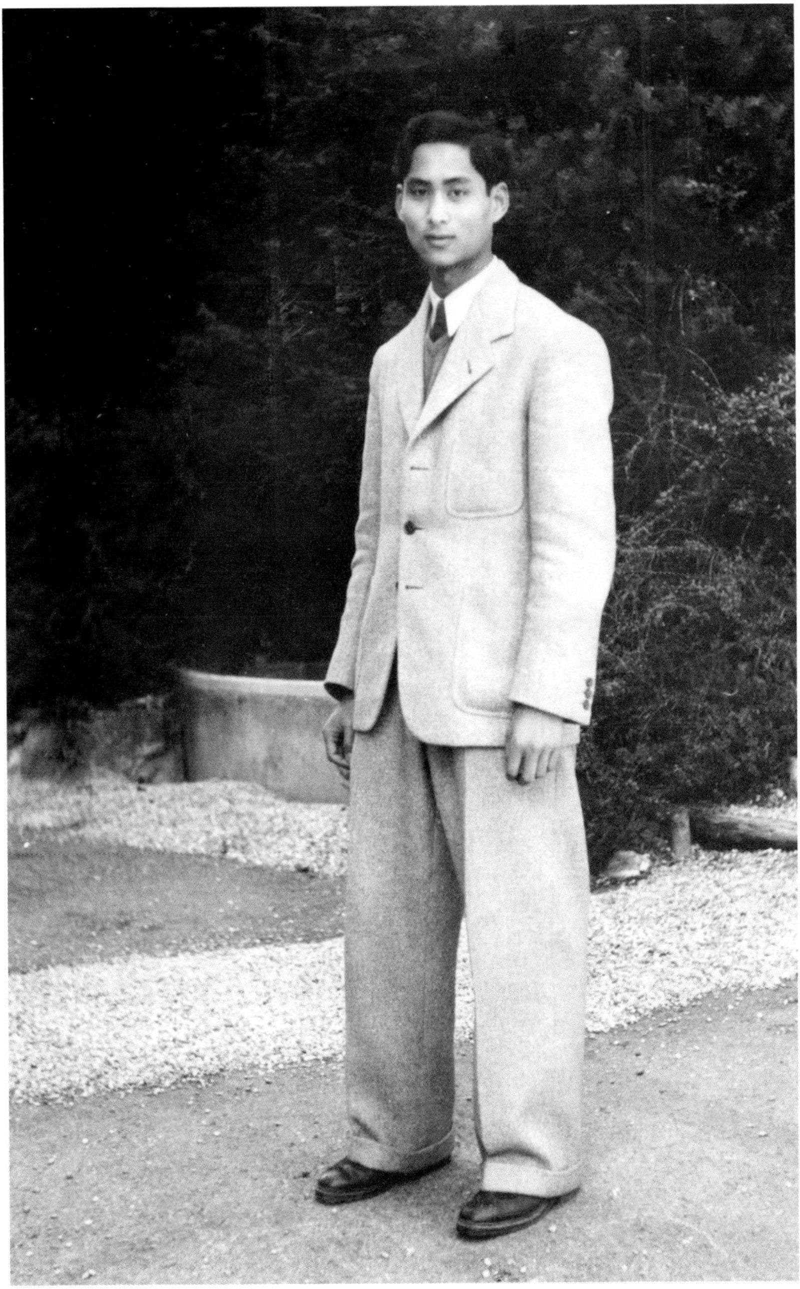

7

TRAGEDY AT THE PALACE

By September 1945, King Ananda was but twenty years of age and faced getting ready for his coronation. His temporary return to Thailand to prepare for this ceremony was organized for the month of December 1945 and the return to Switzerland was to take place at the very beginning of 1946.

Taking the opportunity provided by the Royal Family's absence, Cléon decided to return to the writing of his Ph.D. law thesis, which had been set aside, for the second time, back in 1939 because of his obligations, in order to submit it during this new prolonged absence of the Royal Family.

Upon his departure from Geneva, King Ananda delivered a radio address before leaving for a long flight with many stopovers as aeroplanes of this era tended to be slow and limited range capability.

On 1 December 1945, the King, at the stopover in Cairo, wrote:

My dear Cléon, I don't have time and I cannot write long. The trip has gone well.

Then came observations on occupations and obligations to meet during stopovers. Comments were also made about the plane, a Dakota, described as "wheezing", flying at a speed of 160-170 mph, at an altitude of 6,000 to 9,000 feet. Then some "Arab greetings" (the letter was written in Cairo), with a promise of "Hindu greetings" (at the next stopover in Karachi).

Signed: *Ananda.*

*

At a stopover in Baghdad, Princess Mahidol sent a postcard to Cléon, saying: *We will stay here this evening and will leave tomorrow morning at 8 a.m. for Karachi. Everyone is well. With our best wishes.*

Signed: *S. Mahidol.*

*

3 December 1945

A postcard from Karachi written by King Ananda had a picture of the Taj Mahal Hotel in Bombay, with a remark from the King saying that he wished to visit it but had not done so. He said also that the family would now travel on to Calcutta, perhaps passing through Delhi. He ended with a small hello to the cat and greetings to "[His] dear Cléon".

Signed: *AM.*

*

10 December 1945

Princess Galyani wrote a short letter from Renens to reassure Cléon, saying: *This morning I have received a telegram from mother: "Arrived the 5th. Love to all". Best wishes.*
Signed: *G. Ratanakul.*

*

21 December 1945

Princess Galyani wrote to Cléon, still from Renens, to tell him that she had received letters from her brother Ananda, one from Calcutta, then another mailed at Karachi, which included a personal message for Cléon, saying first that their plane *"had previously welcomed Churchill in the seat occupied by mom!"*, then describing the peoples and places encountered during their long journey from Switzerland.

Their mother had given accounts of the stopover in Cairo, including flying over the pyramids especially for them to see, the high status reception afforded them by the Chamberlain of King Farouk and that a maid had been provided especially to look after the Princess.

Then, on the fourth page of the letter, came greetings from all the family.

*

In the following weeks, personal greeting cards from all the family, then the everyday letters would arrive regularly during the first three months of the year.

Not being able to return as planned, King Ananda wrote to Cléon to give reasons of their prolonged absence:

11 February 1946
Dear Cléon, we wanted to stay here for one month and it is already "doubled" and it is not finished. They wanted us to stay till the opening of Parliament (24 January) and now they would like us to wait till the revision of the Constitution. It is not an amendment but a complete revision. Instead of one chamber there would be two. They say this will take three months, maybe much more.

Our stay goes on but we are not bored. As far as "toys" are concerned we especially have some American equipment: a Jeep; a folding motorcycle for parachutists (the diameter of the wheels is about 25 cm); a walkie-talkie (a transmitting and receiving set with battery that could work for as far as one kilometre) (...). As far as weapons are concerned, we have an entire arsenal:

A "Carline" automatic rifle, 15 shots just by pulling the trigger 15 times; very light and precise.

An American pistol of 11 mm calibre! It makes an enormous noise and I cannot attain any precision.

A "M3" sub-machine gun making 30 shots at 11 mm in a row.

A "Thompson" sub-machine gun, 30 shots as well, but one could shoot like the Carline.

A "Sten" sub-machine gun, a tiny apparatus which, when dismantled, could get into a school bag.

In the country there are quite a number of modern weapons that were parachuted in by the US for the Resistance. The other day we were by the sea and we shot on the bottles that we had thrown out.

As far as the "Resistance" is concerned, there was a widespread underground movement,(...); there were secret airfields where allied agents and weapons were received. Many "relatives" cousins, came down by parachute before Japan surrendered.

There is a large number of problems in the country. (...)

As far as Indochina is concerned, the Allies want the status quo of 1939, at the risk of settling the matter later in a court.

There are huge domestic problems: high inflation, prices have increased ten times, then a hundred times.

There are large numbers of thieves and gangsters. (...) Now the gangsters operate sub-machine guns and grenades.

Clothes are lacking and, in the country, husband and wife sometimes cannot go out together because of the lack of clothes. This is what the country lacks most because food is abundant (not like in neighbouring countries).

Damage caused by bombing is rather small compared to that on Germany. However, the bridges have suffered a lot.

Disorder prevails in the Palace.

We also play music with saxophones: alto, soprano, tenor, clarinet. The ex-Prime Minister and a few musicians come to play with us.

(...)

And the Ratanakuls? Over here, it is not too bad. (...)

As we are not coming back soon, you can write many times. Letters take ten to twenty days to arrive.

Please send on this attached sheet with my fond greetings, and thank you in advance.

There are still many other things. Let me know your preference. Greetings, etc. And to the Ratanakuls!
Signed: *A.M.*

*

On 1 April 1946, Princess Mahidol wrote:
Dear Mr Cléon,
Thank you for your kind letter, I was very pleased to receive news from Tito. I hope he is always behaving well. We get along quite well the three of us. Life over here is interesting, at the same time very tiring. We urgently need an eminent economist to sort out finance.

Life over here is very expansive, a metre of fabric which was 1.50 t now costs 30 to 35 t. The cost of food has also gone up, it is really terrible for modest families. The Kolynos toothpaste is 60 t per tube! The tical is very low. A franc is now worth 6 t. What a life for the Siamese people in Switzerland!

We still do not know when we are going to leave here. I hope that your doctor thesis is moving forward, and that we will soon have a "Doctor". My children and I we send you our friendly wishes, also to your family.
Signed: *S. Mahidol.*

*

On 10 May 1946, on page 20 of the daily newspaper *La Feuille d'Avis de Lausanne*, a Reuters report said that "The King of Siam will return to Switzerland to complete his studies".

16 May 1946

Princess Mahidol sent news to Cléon and told him it was very hot, adding: *Nant puts up with life well here because he has plenty to do in learning a lot of things. Also Lek always finds things to do. He has set up a small workshop next to his bedroom, and he has made a Siamese warship model that he has given to charity to auction and sell. This boat has raised 20,000 tics, to the satisfaction of all,* particularly of his mother, who claims to be proud of her younger son. The letter closes with greetings to Cléon's family, and with a word for Tito, the cat.

20 May 1946

Princess Galyani wrote to Cléon to tell him that the project for the revision of the Constitution by King Ananda was completed. The family still had to stay for the opening of Parliament on 25 May and would go to the United States at the beginning of June for a short official visit, before returning to Switzerland. They all hoped they could leave as anticipated.

*

29 May 1946

The Central Thesis Office in Zurich acknowledged receipt of Cléon's request to defend his thesis in order to obtain his Doctorate in Law. During the absence of the Royal Family he had been able to successfully complete his work on the hitherto unfamiliar field of "Collective Security".

* * *

The tragedy occurred on the morning of 9 June 1946, before dawn: His Majesty King Rama VIII was found dead, killed by a shot from a Colt 45.

Princess Mahidol fainted when she discovered the body of her son. She had to be immediately attended by a doctor called to the Palace. When Princess Galyani was informed, she tried to let Cléon know, but he was absent from his home on a family walk. Upon his return late afternoon he found a note on the door from his neighbour, Mr Kern, saying simply:

Someone phoned us: it's very urgent that Mr Séraïdaris calls back the telephone number 3 14 44, the date and time were written as *10.6.46 / 5 p.m.*

It was therefore by telephone that Princess Galyani told the terrible news to Cléon who, in shock, felt overwhelmed by grief. He immediately sent a telegram of condolence to Princess Mahidol and to Prince Bhumibol. Their reply was telegraphed, saying:

We are deeply touched by your message of condolence and sympathy.

Signed: *Sangwal.*

False stories spread all kind of theories concerning the circumstance of the King's death. The presumed accomplices of this crime were a private secretary and two pages on duty at the Palace. They were judged and then executed on 17 February 1955. Other people suspected of being involved were not immediately uncovered and some, hastily, left the country before they could be tested in court.

Thus, the irreversible had been committed and the Royal Family would never recover from it.

Cléon, who took daily care of Ananda for ten years, would not get over it either. Like the Royal Family, he would remain deeply affected the rest of his life by such a tragic death.

These feelings were owed as much to the personality of the Royal children and of their mother than of Cléon. That explained his devotion to the Royal Family for over twenty-six years.

Similarly, sadness at the sudden death of King Ananda was also deeply felt among his Lausanne entourage, teachers and friends.

"The King is dead. Long live the King!". Whatever one's feelings of the phrase it is an unavoidable fact in most monarchies, and Prince Bhumibol only had a few days to decide to ascend the throne in order to succeed his brother. It was in this way that Prince Bhumibol became King Rama IX of the Chakri Dynasty, formally on 9 June 1946.

On 29 June 1946, the King who had just acceded to the throne, wrote to Cléon on black-edged paper, opening his letter with the following salutation and preamble:

My dear "Sir",

Thank you for your encouraging letter. It is for me, at this time of sorrow and solitude, a great comfort.

The rest, on two pages, were very personal remarks on his feelings and daily occupations. The King explained he did not then know when he would return to Switzerland. There were the ceremonies for "Nant", then he listed the ways he employed to assist him cope with his grief, admitting he had difficulty in accepting the reality of his brother's death. He asked Cléon to write to him again.

In the envelope he placed the last photograph he took of his brother, on the occasion of a visit to the University of Agriculture, near Bangkok.

The King signed the letter to his tutor with a signature that is particularity moving:

From your friend Pumipol.

His Majesty King Rama VIII

The King, accompanied by the Princess Mother and the tutor,
attends a League of Nations conference in Geneva, 1945

King Ananda in Vadhana Villa's garden with Princess Galyani,
then with Cléon

October 1945

In Vadhana Villa's garden

Geneva airport. King Ananda delivers a radio address before heading to Bangkok

Arrival in Bangkok in December 1945

Visit of an experimental farming station in Bangkok.
The last official duty of King Rama VIII in the spring of 1946

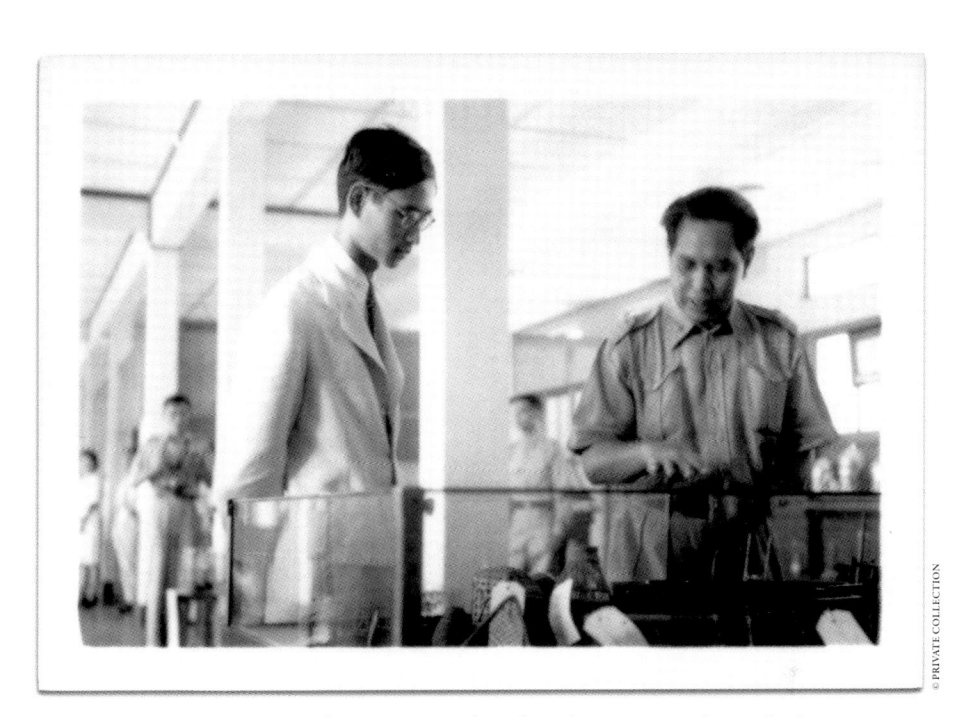

Last picture of King Ananda taken by Prince Bhumibol

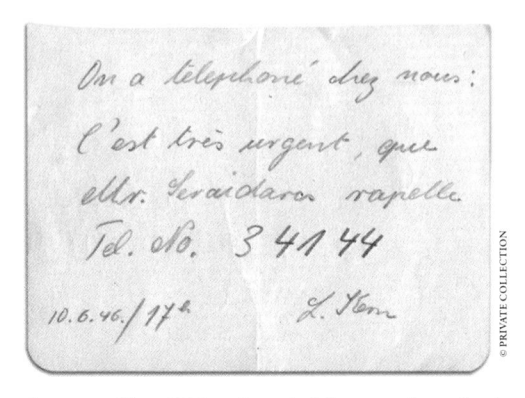

The note dropped by Cléon's neighbour when he had to be
informed about the tragedy that had just happened in the Palace

= SERAIDARIS MONTCHOISI LAUSANNE

= NOUS SOMMES PROFONDEMENT TOUCHES PAR VOTRE MESAGE

CONDOLEANCES ET DE SYMPTHIE = SANGWALYA +

CT SANGWALYA

The telegram sent to Cléon by Princess Mahidol

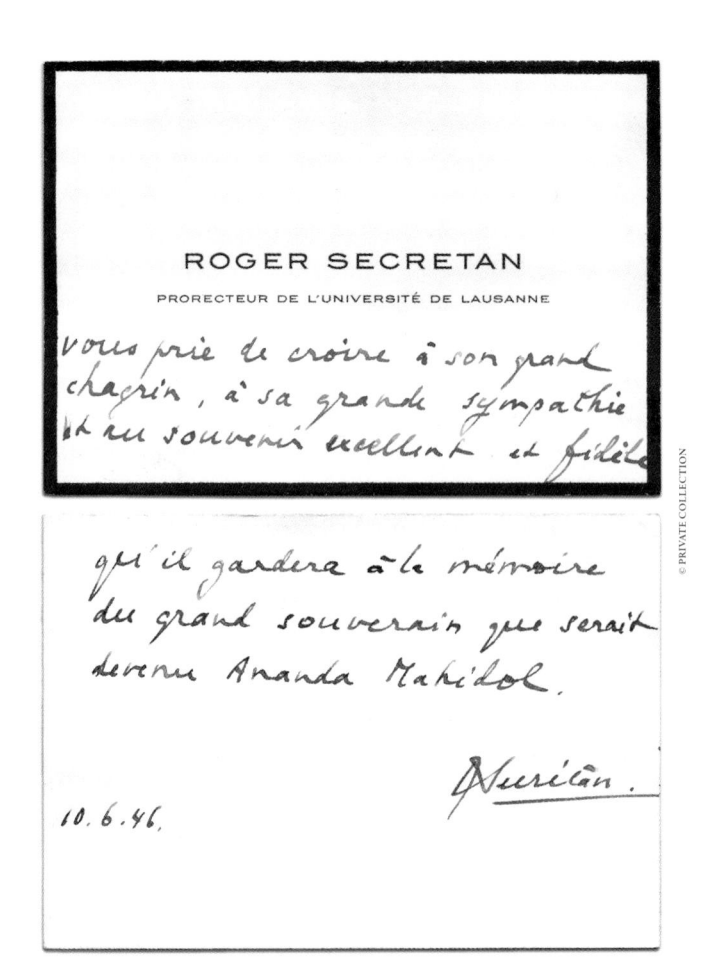

Sympathy card from the University of Lausanne's prorector

Translation :

ROGER SECRETAN
PRORECTOR OF THE UNIVERSITY OF LAUSANNE

with great sorrow offers his deepest sympathy and maintains fond recollections that will keep alive the memory of the great sovereign that Ananda Mahidol would have become.
R. Secrétan
10.6.46

ECOLE NOUVELLE
CHAILLY sur LAUSANNE

Association
des
Anciens Elèves

FÉVRIER 1947

L. GENEUX, LAUSANNE

Above and next pages: bulletin from *École Nouvelle* in Chailly published in memory of His Majesty King Rama VIII

Ananda Mahidol

1925—1946.

Le 9 juin 1946, nous apprenions avec stupeur, par la radio, la mort de Sa Majesté le Roi de Siam Ananda Mahidol, mystérieusement tué d'une balle en son palais de Bangkok. Des rapports officiels, confus et contradictoires, parlaient d'accident et étaient susceptibles d'égarer l'opinion publique par des bruits fantaisistes. Cependant, l'enquête judiciaire, les rapports des médecins et des personnes qui étaient sur place concluent à un assassinat commis pendant le sommeil du jeune roi.

— 13 —

La disparition d'Ananda Mahidol est un chagrin immense pour sa famille qui l'adorait. Nous pensons à elle avec une profonde sympathie, et particulièrement à sa mère. Pendant vingt ans, elle s'est donnée entièrement à l'éducation de ses enfants et c'est au moment de recueillir la récompense de son effort qu'elle se voit douloureusement frappée.

Le Siam perd un souverain intelligent, foncièrement honnête et bon, qui aurait pu faire beaucoup pour son pays. En six mois de présence, sa personnalité sympathique avait réussi à refaire l'unité de la nation, fortement ébranlée par la guerre et les privations.

Nous aussi, nous éprouvons une grande tristesse. Nous perdons en Ananda le meilleur des camarades. Ses professeurs étaient unanimes à louer ses qualités intellectuelles et morales : un garçon magnifiquement équilibré, avec un sens du devoir hors ligne.

Après avoir suivi pendant huit ans les classes de l'Ecole, Ananda avait fait, en 1943, un excellent baccalauréat. Ses progrès s'affirmaient à l'Université. Il venait de passer brillamment les examens de la première partie de son doctorat en droit quand il estima que sa présence à Bangkok était nécessaire à son pays. Il devait revenir au milieu de juin. Son intention était de terminer ses études, de présenter une thèse en sciences juridiques, puis de s'instruire encore en voyageant afin d'être le plus utile possible à la communauté de ses dix-huit millions de sujets.

C'est avec émotion que nous voyons sa lourde charge revenir dès maintenant à son frère Pumipol. Nous savons le courage, la claire vision des réalités avec lesquels celui-ci l'a assumée. Nous lui présentons, avec respect et affection, nos vœux ardents pour un règne heureux.

Nous voudrions, au nom de l'Ecole nouvelle, dire ici notre reconnaissance à la Princesse Mahidol pour la confiance qu'elle nous a toujours témoignée et notre gratitude pour l'aide qu'elle et ses enfants ont apportée à notre institution pendant les mauvais moments de la guerre.

Que la famille d'Ananda Mahidol trouve ici l'expression de nos meilleures pensées.

ÉCOLE NOUVELLE
Chailly-sur-Lausanne

ASSOCIATION OF ALUMNI

February 1947

Ananda Mahidol
1925 – 1946

On 9 June 1946, we were shocked to hear, on the radio, about the death of His Majesty the King of Siam, Ananda Mahidol, mysteriously shot and killed in his Bangkok palace. Confused and contradictory official reports spoke of an accident and were likely to mislead public opinion by fanciful rumours. However, the judicial enquiry and reports from physicians and persons who were there concluded that an assassination was committed while the young king was asleep.

The disappearance of Ananda Mahidol is a profound sorrow for his family who adored him. We think of them with great sympathy, and especially his mother. For twenty years she dedicated herself entirely to educating her children and now that the time has come to reap the benefit of her efforts she has been cruelly hit.

Siam has lost an intelligent, honest and good sovereign, who could have done a lot for his country. After a presence of just six months, his friendly personality succeeded in restoring the unity of the nation, badly shaken by war and deprivation.

Translation of the bulletin from *École Nouvelle* in Chailly

We ourselves also feel a great sadness. In Ananda, we have lost the best of friends. His teachers were unanimous in praising his intellectual and moral qualities: a supremely well-balanced young man, with an outstanding sense of duty.

After attending the École Nouvelle classes for eight years, Ananda successfully passed the baccalaureate in 1943. His progress continued at the university. He had just brilliantly passed the examinations for the first part of his Doctorate in Law when he considered that his presence in Bangkok was necessary for his country. He was to return in the middle of June. His intention was to finish studying, to present a thesis in juridical sciences and to educate himself even more by travelling in order to be as useful as possible to his community of 18 million of subjects.

It is with emotion that we see that this heavy burden now falls on his brother Pumipol. We understand the courage, the clear vision of reality with which he has assumed it. We offer him, with respect and affection, our fervent wishes for a happy reign.

We would like, on behalf of the École Nouvelle, to offer our gratitude to Princess Mahidol for the confidence she always shown us and for the help she and her children gave to our institution during the bad times of the war.

We offer the Ananda Mahidol family our very deepest thoughts.

8

RETURN TO LAUSANNE
TO FINISH STUDIES

O n 19 August 1946, just after the official formalities relating to the late King had been completed, the Royal Family returned to Switzerland. As soon as he arrived in Lausanne the King set aside his scientific studies to study law.

This had therefore repercussions on the future of Cléon since he no longer had time available to defend his doctoral thesis. New tasks related to the essential legal education required by King Rama IX became his highest priority.

HM King Bhumibol was to recall this during a private audience granted to the author in 2003, the King adding that he had never forgotten his tutor's sacrifice, and that he retained a deep sense of gratitude toward him.

Family life was no longer the same as it had been at Vadhana Villa and security had to be drastically reinforced. Cléon, who loathed firearms, had to carry one during the first few months upon the King's return to Lausanne. Later, a little while before his return to Thailand, the King decided to acquire two Boxer dogs intended to stand guard. They proved to be as ferocious as they were trained to be.

Fifty years on, at a private audience, His Majesty asked the author if he recalled the Boxer dogs. Indeed how could he forget the fear these two animals engendered. They were tall and large as he was at five years of age. The King added that Cléon also admitted the dogs made him uneasy. Kindly, the King confided in Lysandre that these two "guards" did not make him feel at ease either. In 1951, these two watchdogs were transferred to stand guard at the private apartments in the Palace at Hua Hin.

The guard dogs being in the Vadhana Villa meant that Tito, the King's Siamese cat, had to be removed as he would not admit the dogs to his territory and it was feared the dogs would make short work of him. Tito was re-homed with Cléon's family and later took up residence with a very dear friend of the Royal Family who lived in Martigny, where their care and the availability of a large garden enabled Tito to live into the late 1950s, attaining a respectable age.

The King and his tutor at that time still retained a liking for cats but much later both transferred their affection to their own dog as a new lifelong friend.

* * *

To mark the many happy years the Royal Family had enjoyed at *Chamblandes*, it was decided in 1945 to finance the construction of a large chalet to house the children from Pully for summer camps. It was fact that, at that time, few children took holidays. Therefore, the project to donate a modern rural summer camp for the local children's use was received with joy by the Pully authorities. They made available a piece of land up in the country village of the Monts-de-Pully.

The building was opened on 9 July 1946 in the presence of General Guisan and the first children who came to stay there. In regular use since then, the chalet underwent a major re-vamp in the 1970s and was made available as a summer camp for children from neighbouring countries and to local associations to rent and organize festive events there.

HM King Bhumibol together with HRH Princess Mahidol and HRH Princess Galyani in mourning welcomed by Cléon at Geneva airport when returning to Switzerland after the tragedy, August 1946

ALL RIGHTS RESERVED

King Bhumibol and Cléon riding a folding US Army Parachutist motorcycle received in Bangkok in the spring of 1946

The Chalet of *Bois-du-Moulin* offered to the school children of Pully thanks to the Royal Family's generous donation

The King performs one of his jazz compositions accompanied at the clarinet by young Khun Prija Bahiddha-Nukara, colloquially known as "Peter". Son of the Ambassador of Thailand at the time, he was studying at the University of Lausanne along with His Majesty

9

AUTOMOTIVE INTERLUDE

The delivery to the Royal Family of a magnificent Mercedes-Benz 500 Nürburg Landaulet in October 1935 aroused in Ananda and Bhumibol their first interest in mechanics and automobiles. This very large car needed to be chauffeur driven. In 1939 the Mercedes was replaced by an equally large Delahaye limousine, then later by other Salmson cars better suited to driving in Lausanne.

During the war there were very few motor vehicles on the roads. The young King and Prince could therefore, safely, go for long bicycle rides, accompanied by their tutor. One such popular ride was to visit Jacques Piccard, son of Professor Auguste Piccard, the celebrated Swiss physicist. Jacques Piccard was later to become a world renowned oceanographer, holder in 1960 of the deep-sea diving depth record, for having piloted the bathyscaphe *Trieste* designed by his father. Throughout his life Jacques Piccard, a doctor *honoris causa*, remained a faithful friend to the King.

Other Sunday excursions included car trips to Geneva for lunch at the *Palais Impérial, Rue de la Tour-Maîtresse*, then the very first Chinese restaurant opened in Switzerland. It was managed by a former apprentice Chef at the Imperial Court of China. Some forty years later, the Chef's wife fondly recalled the magnificent basket of cherries the young sovereign brought for her, picked at the Vadhana Villa.

* * *

In 1947, Princess Mahidol acquired another Salmson, an elegant sky-blue convertible. King Bhumibol insisted on having a dark green Fiat Topolino. He found the little car entertaining and a nice drive. The King loved the Topolino so much that he tuned the engine and would wash the car himself in the garden of the villa. This car, full of charm, became one of his hobbies.

* * *

In October 1949, as in 1947, the Automobile Grand Prix of Lausanne took place at *La Blécherette* racing circuit. "Grand Prix", until the 1950s, corresponded to the current "Formula 1" (this last name was adopted at the beginning of the 1950s). The King was particularly interested because his cousin, Prince Bira, was a well-known racing driver who had won the Gold Star of the BRDC (British Racing Drivers' Club) for three consecutive years, in 1936, 1937 and 1938. Bira probably encouraged his cousin Bhumibol's interest in sports cars and in driving them, even though with his brother, King Rama VIII, he had been interested, since early childhood, in this great technological development that was the automobile during the 20th century.

Prince Birabongse Bhanudej Bhanubandh maintained a relationship of great warmth and friendship with Cléon while making himself known for his exploits in the grands prix and the automotive world under the name of Bira, no doubt believing his usual name may be difficult for the western public to remember. Grandson of King Mongkut, King Rama IV, Bira, an orphan, was pupil of Prince Chula Chakrabongse, an enthusiast of car racing who founded his own racing team in the colours of Siam. This private team received the nickname of "White Mouse", an allusion to the white elephant shown on the flag of the Kingdom of Siam before Constitutional changes and with reference to the small mouse synonymous of speed and modesty in Thai language. Prince Chula equipped his team, Bira being the main driver, with three ERA cars, short name for English Racing Automobiles. Built with Riley engines, these were exceptionally strong and well running, mounted on a light steel frame, efficient and for the time somewhat revolutionary in design. The three cars, just like racing horses, received the symbolic names of Romulus and Remus, founders of the City of Rome, and of Hanuman, the mythological hero, inseparable companion of Prince Rama in the Siamese traditional theatre. These three models had different engines, but the best performing one was the 1,500 cc with which Bira became famous during many grands prix before war, and was champion for three consecutive years in 1936, 1937 and 1938. He won among others the Grand Prix of Monaco in 1936.

Bira lived in England, and travelled by piloting his own plane, while his cars were transported on trucks. On his flights to Lausanne he landed at *La Blécherette* airfield.

When motor racing restarted after the war, Bira was no longer as successful as he had been in the previous decade, not only because he was now thirty-five years old and had been out of practice throughout the war years but also because he was now faced with competition from "factory" stables which deployed much larger budgets than a private racing stable with a couple of racing drivers.

At the Grand Prix of Lausanne in 1947 and 1949, the King of Thailand found himself in the company of the elite of Europe: Prince Baudouin of Belgium, who was not yet King, Prince Rainier of Monaco and Prince Vittorio Emanuele of Italy, all of whom were passionate about motor racing.

At the 1949 Grand Prix Bira took the start with a Maserati 4 CLT. He also distinguished himself driving the small-engined Simca-Gordini at other races. At the beginning of the 1950s, Cléon and his eldest son Léandre accompanied Bira to Bologna, Italy, to visit the O.S.C.A. workshops founded by the Maserati brothers. Bira wanted to have his 4 CLT tuned, which was then tested on the Monza circuit. Bira also owned one of the only two Maserati 12 cylinder prototypes, one of which is now in the private collection of the Prince of Monaco.

Bira retired from racing in the middle of the 1950s and returned to Thailand where he devoted himself to flying and the import of cars. Passing into relative obscurity, Bira died in London in 1985 toward the end of the year.

Few years ago, Remus, one of the three ERA cars was put on sale in London for almost half a million pounds sterling.

The memory of this prince, the first and talented Thai racing driver is in name perpetuated at the "Bira International Circuit" not far from Pattaya. It is there that promising young Thai drivers come to develop their racing skills, as well as go-karting on a second track built more recently.

* * *

On 4 October 1948 King Bhumibol and his sister Princess Galyani's husband, Khun Aram Ratanakul, decided to drive into Geneva, in the Fiat Topolino to attend a jazz concert. His tutor had expressed reservations as to using such a small vehicle outside the city and would have preferred they take one of the larger cars for safety reasons but they would not be deterred.

Nonetheless, at about 9 p.m. the King and his brother-in-law set off for Geneva in the Topolino taking the old national road, today known as *Route du Lac*, then the only direct link between Lausanne and Geneva.

They wanted to reach Geneva as fast as possible, although the notion of speed with this car was relative because the Topolino's small 500 cc with rear-wheel drive developed only 16 hp engine and would have struggled to achieve 50 mph, a speed considered fast. This was one of the deficiencies in the matter of safety.

Around 9.45 p.m. on the slope from Préverenges toward Morges, the King suddenly saw in front of him an old truck with defective rear lights slowing down. He wanted to overtake but at just that moment he was dazzled by the headlights of an oncoming car, bearing down on him with full headlights.

Sensibly the King decided to brake and pull back behind the truck which then fiercely braked for pedestrians in the road.

The wheels of the small car locked and went into a skid and the collision with the rear end of the truck was inevitable. The left rear corner of the truck smashed through the windscreen and into the compartment.

Both occupants were seriously wounded. At that time, no ambulance service was available but transport was rapidly arranged and both men were taken to the old hospital at Morges by taxi.

The King suffered concussion (seat belts did not exist then) and his condition becoming worrying, he was shortly transferred to a private clinic in Lausanne. It was during his stay there that he had the opportunity to become better acquainted with his future Queen, Mom Rajawongse Sirikit Kittiyakara, who had rushed from Paris to his bedside and then extended her stay in Switzerland to assist him during his convalescence.

* * *

The role of private tutor was not only to supervise the studies but also, after the first ten years of duty, to act as personal advisor. During the year 1949, the King maintained a perfect discretion about the visits he made to neighbouring cantons. He did not wish to disclose the places he was visiting. Thus, accompanied by his tutor, the only person he fully trusted, he would set off on "private excursions" in the Salmson car. The speed and rapid acceleration of this car often enabled the King to outsmart the Canton of Vaud Security Police and escape from their protective surveillance. The police didn't necessarily realize the true reason for these sudden bursts of speed and so they were often reported as "sporting prowesses".

* * *

The King's gratitude toward Cléon was such as to offer him a superb green two-tone MG saloon as a gift. It was arranged for the MG to carry the same registration number as the now abandoned Topolino.

The gift delighted Cléon and his wife who for fifteen years took pleasure in driving the MG.

* * *

The Royal family often went to Oyonnax, in the French Department of Ain, where the King had particular interest in the new technologies used in the vanguard plastics factory there and in the promising possibilities of developing them in his Kingdom. The road from Geneva to Lyon no longer held any secrets for the tutor, who drove the car himself while on these trips.

On 5 November 1949, Cléon, accompanied by Princess Mahidol, left early in the morning in the Princess's Salmson convertible to go to the Lyon region. At about 10.30 a.m., at a curve near Nantua, they found themselves facing an oncoming truck being driven on the wrong side of the road. Despite Cléon's vigorous braking, the collision could not be avoided. The truck occupied the entire roadway alongside a railway.

Princess Mahidol was injured, as was Cléon. The injuries sustained were not serious, but necessitated hospitalization and both the Princess and Cléon suffered after-effects for many years.

As an anecdote, the French authorities, thoughtful as to the respect of the distinguished guests who visited the territory of the Republic, interceded with the offender's insurance company in order to replace without delay the royal car which was out of use. The Salmson factory located at Boulogne-Billancourt near Paris rapidly provided a new replacement car. This time it was a four-door saloon, smaller and less luxurious. Convertibles were hand-built to order and would have entailed a long delivery time.

The Mercedes-Benz Nürburg previously owned by the Royal Family and recently found in Switzerland

One of the Salmsons

Bira on board of one of his ERAs in 1946

King Bhumibol comes to support Bira in the stands
at the Grand Prix of Lausanne

King Bhumibol with Prince Rainier of Monaco,
young Prince Vittorio Emanuele of Italy and Mr Jacques Piccard

Bira giving his last instructions to his mechanic
at the Grand Prix of Lausanne

Bira in Monza with his Maserati

Receipt of payment concerning the reparation of Bira's 4 CLT
signed by one of the Maserati brothers

Translation :

Cars
O.S.C.A.
                                                                                  Bologna, 19.10.1950

                    Mr Cléon C. Séraïdaris
                    Tutor to HM the King of Siam
                    51, Chamblandes-dessus
                    Lausanne (Switzerland)

We acknowledge receipt of your letter of the 16th of this month and thank you for the information provided.

Meanwhile, we are awaiting a corresponding communication from the bank in order to start the repairs to Prince Bira's car.

With best regards,

                                    O.S.C.A.
                                    Technical Office
                                    Maserati Bindo

Cléon in Monza with Bira's Maserati

The entrance gate of Bira International Circuit in Pattaya

Bira's bust at the circuit entry

Commemorative plate for Bira's three victories in 1936, 1937 and 1938 at the BRDC Road Racing Gold Star. Underneath, Bira's signature decorates the monument's pedestal

The go-kart circuit where young racers train

King Bhumibol with his Fiat Topolino

Re-enactment of the accident with the Topolino.
It shows the lighting fault of the truck

Re-enactment of the accident in Nantua
with the smaller replacement Salmson

The damaged Salmson

10

ROLE OF THE PERSONAL PAGES

The Princess Mother decided that two personal pages, Kaewkhwan and Khwankeo Vajarodaya, should go to Switzerland to act as pages to the King. There the pages would have training and gain experience in the western working methods that the King wished to develop in Thailand. Their studies were offered by the Princess.

These twin brothers came from a noble family who served the Royal Dynasty over several generations. They acceded to the highest offices in the Kingdom, having been, since their seventeenth year of age, devoted and loyal key persons permanently on duty close to His Majesty.

When the twins were still young men, they were appointed to be photographers to the King. The retired Lausanne photographer, Albert Barras, who had taken over Photo-Ciné Rich, his uncle's shop at *Rue de la Grotte*, still remembers the two Vajarodaya brothers very well, welcome customers for many years.

Kaewkhwan, who studied at the State of Fribourg Agricultural Institute, became Lord Chamberlain, in charge of finance and rural and industrial development projects. These tasks were essential for the modernization strategy of the vast rural regions of the Kingdom.

As for Khwankeo, he was appointed Grand Chamberlain, Head of the Royal Household, which included the important and often delicate duties and responsibilities of organizing receptions honouring foreign Heads of State on their official visits to the Kingdom.

He was eminently qualified in these responsibilities as his academic path in Lausanne comprised the *Champittet* College, the Graduate School of Business and recipient of a diploma with honours from *École Hôtelière*. Later in 1993 he became Honorary *Stammvater* in Bangkok (President of the local Association of Alumni) and then in 2010 was awarded the title of EHL Honorary Professor.

At the beginning of the King's reign, Khwankeo also carried out the duties of Director of AS Radio, a private broadcasting station belonging to the King, located at Dusit Palace. The Station's aims were to encourage mobilization of people around their King in supporting the underprivileged in the rural or urban areas, especially those affected by natural disasters, such as the floods and tornadoes that often afflict the Northern and Eastern parts of the Kingdom.

The principle, familiar to listeners to *Radio Suisse Romande*, the French-speaking Swiss radio, was not only to give news of the affected areas, but to collect funds to deal quickly with the need for food, shelter and medicine. Instructed by His

Majesty, the station, under the Directorship of HE Khwankeo Vajarodaya provided interactive music programmes, during which listeners could request songs and music and dedicate these to people of their choice, while making donations to disaster victims. These transmissions were a great success with the people, traditionally and fundamentally inclined to show solidarity with their fellow countrymen in need of their generosity.

Among the too frequent examples of natural disasters that confirmed the usefulness of AS Radio is the devastation caused by the tropical storm Harriet that swept in and severely damaged Nakhon Si Thammarat and dozens of other Southern province locations in 1962. The AS Radio played a vital role in seeking for the solidarity of the people who felt it a duty to contribute to the aid initiated by the King.

This same movement of solidarity encouraged by AS Radio brought about an efficient fight against leprosy, cholera and poliomyelitis. This episode is mentioned in chapter 14. Such action was also key following the dramatic *tsunami* which struck South Asia on 26 December 2004. One could say that the AS Radio private station continues to foster a strong bond between the people and the King.

As of 1991 HE Khwankeo Vajarodaya will be President of the Rajaprajanugroh Foundation, the name literally meaning "Mutual help and support *(anugroh)* between the King *(raja)* and the people *(praja)*". This Foundation gives immediate help to victims following a natural disaster event. Furthermore, the Foundation gives care to orphans through education, helping them to build their future. This is a major theme in the development of the Kingdom desired and initiated by the King.

HE Khwankeo Vajarodaya also acts as President of the most important royal philanthropic organizations and is Director of the Royal School of Klai Kang Won, in Hua Hin, which has more than two thousand students. He is also the Director of the Foundation for Distance Learning, based in Bangkok but transmitting from Hua Hin.

HRH Princess Galyani in conversation with
Kaewkhwan and Khwankeo

Kaewkhwan and Khwankeo Vajarodaya in Lausanne, 1947

Thanpuying Pensri Vajarodaya and HE Khun Kaewkhwan Vajarodaya,
HE Khun Khwankeo Vajarodaya and Thanpuying Wattana Vajarodaya

11

KING RAMA IX

When HM King Bhumibol acceded to the throne, after the tragic events of 9 June 1946, he returned to Lausanne to continue his studies.

His first intent was to register at the Faculty of Law at the University of Lausanne, following the advice of his tutor. Indeed the young King was aware that a Head of State must have a solid legal knowledge as an asset to meet his responsibilities.

In his later years of study in Switzerland between the end of 1946 and December 1951, the King travelled extensively to many European countries, with his duties in mind. He therefore established necessary and useful relations and contacts with a number of European monarchies and republics as well as with the political personalities in command in their recently war-torn countries. His tutor always accompanied him, even on private outings.

Sometimes, he travelled incognito. Some for this purpose the King pretended he was his tutor's son. However, during on such stay in Paris the tutor learned that the French *Sécurité* were not to be deceived, when in an informal discussion Mr Séraïdaris was asked by a high ranking French official to convey respectful compliments to "his son"...

* * *

In the spring of 1950, two important and happy royal events took place: the King's wedding on 28 April and his coronation on 5 May at a grandiose ceremony in Bangkok.

For the wedding, special jewels had to be designed for the new Queen. Two prestigious Paris jewellers were asked to submit designs and because the Royal Family resided there, a Lausanne jeweller was asked also. After various designs were examined, creations of André Grumser, of Lausanne, were selected.

* * *

Toward the end of February 1950, King Bhumibol and his *fiancée*, Mom Rajawongse Sirikit went to Thailand to celebrate their marriage and to organize the coronation ceremonies. They travelled by train from Bellegarde (France) to Nice then at Villefranche Bay sailed on the *M/S Selandia*, a Danish ship.

The King had with him, on board, two cars that he had recently purchased for use in Hua Hin. One was a Delahaye convertible, the other a Simca sport convertible, both went on board at Nice before the arrival of the royal delegation.

On 2 March 1950, off Crete, the King wrote a letter to his tutor to be posted from Port Said the next day. He noted that the food on board was excellent and that he could look to gain weight which would be reserves needed for the coming weeks expected to be so full of ceremonies and events such he would not have time for meals.

Other letters followed, from Suez and Colombo telling of life on board and making observations.

On 14 March 1950, on board of the *Selandia*, the King writes to Cléon to update him about his life on board. He mentions in his letter that the weather is terribly hot and that he's swimming in the *Selandia's* pool, so salty one could almost float. He says how he was happy to spot dolphins swimming and jumping around the ship just as they arrived in Aden. He took shots of these with his 8 mm camera. He regretted however not having had the opportunity to see and film whales.

They went ashore in Aden on 8 March at about 5 p.m. The King described on half a page the reception given by the Government of Aden the following day, especially mentioning the guests present, including the local chief of police, who resembled Deputy-Sergeant Fellay, the Canton of Vaud Security Police guard at Vadhana Villa. Except the Aden version was more portly!

There followed comments on the common security problems faced locally by the authorities of Aden and their relationships with the various ethnic groups that lived there.

The *Selandia*, having taken on fuel, it being less expensive in Aden, put sea at midnight on 9 March, heading for Colombo.

On 11 March to celebrate the birthday of King Frederick IX of Denmark, the *Selandia's* captain offered a cocktail party, dinner and dancing on the bridge, in honour of his sovereign. The King added that they would arrive in Colombo harbour during the evening of 14 March, to be received ashore the next morning at about 9 a.m. Following the welcoming ceremony, they would take luncheon with the Minister of Transport standing in for the Prime Minister, currently on a trip, before coming back on board by 3 p.m.

The King promises to give some news from Colombo because, at the moment, it's just too hot on this boat to write!

A letter, dated 21 March 1950, was written from Bukit Serene, the residence in Singapore of Sir Malcolm McDonald, High Commissioner-General, giving some details. On approaching Singapore, at 11 a.m., a barge came out to the *Selandia*, carrying the Siamese Minister of Foreign Affairs and the Palace Grand Chamberlain, bringing them to arrange matters for the official arrival at the quay of His Majesty. There, the Governor waited with a military band and a company of about hundred guards which the King, on landing, reviewed with the Governor. Then followed the presentation of the authorities and other personalities in office at Singapore.

Then the King was invited to enter a Rolls-Royce for a ride of approximately 18 miles over relatively good, but narrow, roads.

The King, being knowledgeable about motor-mechanicals, noticed, in passing, that the suspension of the Rolls-Royce was somewhat worn as it swung abnormally and that the ignition was not properly set, incurring noisy "bangs" from the exhaust, this all from a motorcar renowned for its silent running…

At 1 p.m. they arrived at the residence of Sir Malcolm whose title of High Commissioner-General was equivalent to the status of Governor-General of Malaysia.

At 6.30 p.m. the King was taken to the Consulate General of Siam, where a dinner of Chinese delicacies was served at a meal lasting over two hours. The King also had a few things brought to him at the Consulate and he bought a fountain pen with reservoir and an Eversharp pencil, as well as a Contax telephoto 80 mm f/1:2 camera, and a viewfinder. Close to midnight a car took him back to Bukit Serene.

The King continued in his letter explaining to his tutor that he had not either written from Colombo as promised nor from the ship, because he had a very bad headache on board, possibly because of the excessive heat. Fortunately, the pain had gone following a torrential rainstorm which cleared the air. He therefore now was able to return his mind to the detail of the stopover at Colombo. It was fortuitous that the King was welcomed by the Minister of Transport, the most important person in the Cabinet after the Prime Minister. As Minister responsible for the railways, civil aviation and road construction, he said his department spent half the Government budget! The King found him cheerful and full of humour…

After having berthed at 9 a.m. the delegated Minister had immediately taken the King to the Prime Minister's residence where he was pleased to be welcomed, on behalf of the latter's absence, by his wife.

At 10.30 a.m. without the Minister of Transport, they went to the Buddhist Temple, where the people gave them a welcome qualified as "tremendous". The King proceeded across a symbolic white floor-covering to the opening of a new gallery of pictures and carvings representing the life of the Buddha.

Then prizes were distributed at a primary school to children who had passed examinations. There followed the traditional speeches and replies. These events were clearly a great success.

At noon a champagne reception was held at the residence of the Minister of Transport, followed by a Singhalese meal, comprising rice and curry, traditional dishes of dried fish, chicken dishes, spicy sauces and many other local delicacies.

At 3.30 p.m. the King and his entourage returned to the *Selandia* that cast off at 4 p.m. The King was touched by the warm and friendly reception extended to him by the authorities and people in all the countries he made stopovers, putting him at ease everywhere, and believed it augured well for future relations.

The King informed his tutor that he had already finished his seventh 8 mm film at Colombo and that he would have ten more to develop after Singapore. He closed this letter saying his next one would be written from Bangkok.

In a few lines sent on 27 March 1950 from Bangkok the King told his tutor that he already felt over-busy as there were many ceremonies and long speeches every day.

He mentioned that the cars had suffered on the long sea journey, with a bump on the wing of the Simca and salt-rust in its distributor-head as on the body of the Delahaye, all despite them being packed carefully in wooden crates.

Then came an important message: the King asked Cléon to kindly inform the Princess Mother that Princess Galyani was, once again, entitled to use the style and title of Royal Princess, as he had just signed, together with the Prime Minister, the Royal Decree restoring what she had lost when marrying Colonel Aram Ratanakul while in Switzerland.

The King added news that, on 24 March, he had assumed the title of Marshal of the Royal Navy and on 26 March, the title of Marshall of the Air-Force. There were many details of ceremonies and speeches which the King would give later, but he stressed that at present he had a heavy workload.

On 28 April 1950, the wedding ceremony took place at the Grand Palace in the presence of the most important dignitaries of the Kingdom.

On 5 May 1950, the coronation ceremony and celebration took place in the throne room of the Grand Palace, while outside thousands of Thais gathered since before dawn waited along the route of the royal procession, hoping to catch a glimpse of the King and to express their joy in having a newly-crowned sovereign. Indeed, since the abdication of King Rama VII in 1932, his successor, His Majesty King Rama VIII could not be crowned.

According to protocol, the master of ceremonies gave the crown to the King, who placed it himself on his head because no one else has the right to do so. Then, his young wife knelt before him as he bestowed on her the sacred royal insignia due her as Queen. After giving his first public speech as anointed King Rama IX in which he solemnly pledged to rule with rigor and justice, the royal couple were cheered by the assembled jubilant throng. Newspapers throughout the world dedicated full pages telling of the coronation.

Later the King and the Queen would return to Lausanne to enable the King to finish his studies.

The King and the Queen in their Delahaye at Vadhana Villa

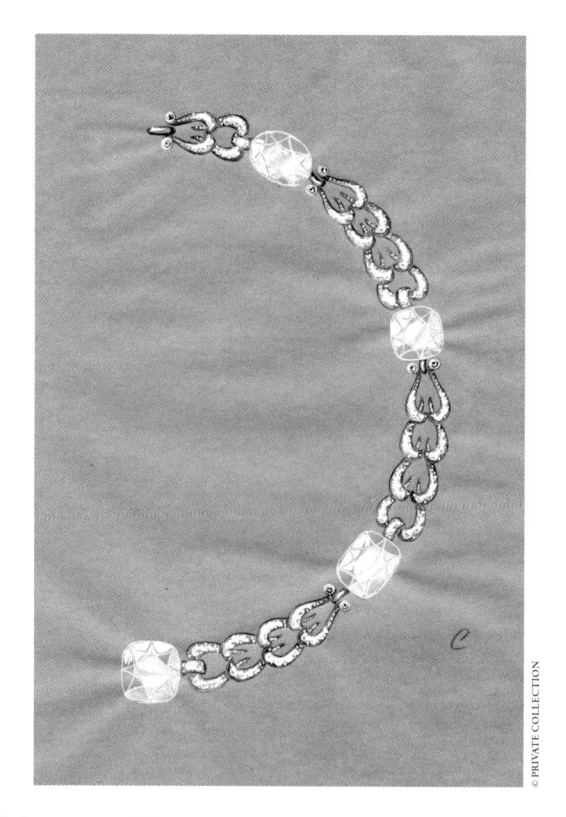

Original drawings of the jewels designed by the Lausanne jeweller...

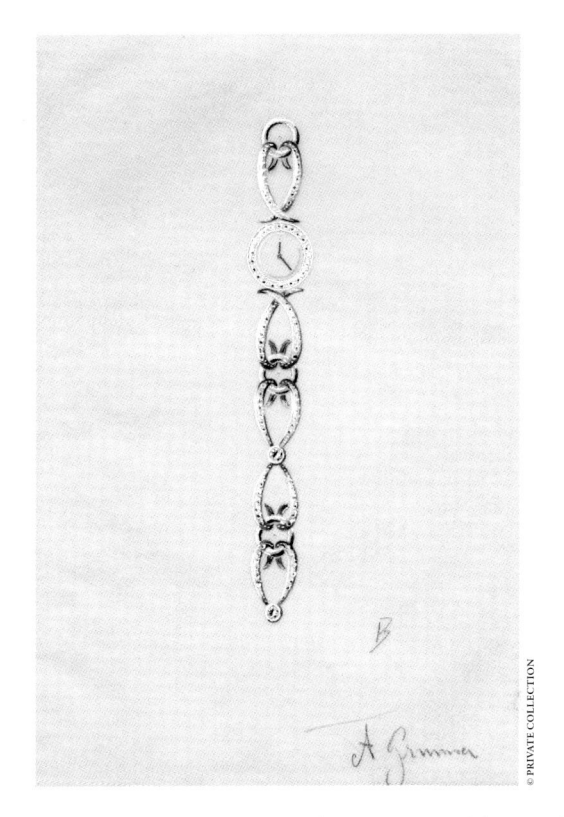

… André Grumser for Queen Sirikit on the occasion of the royal wedding

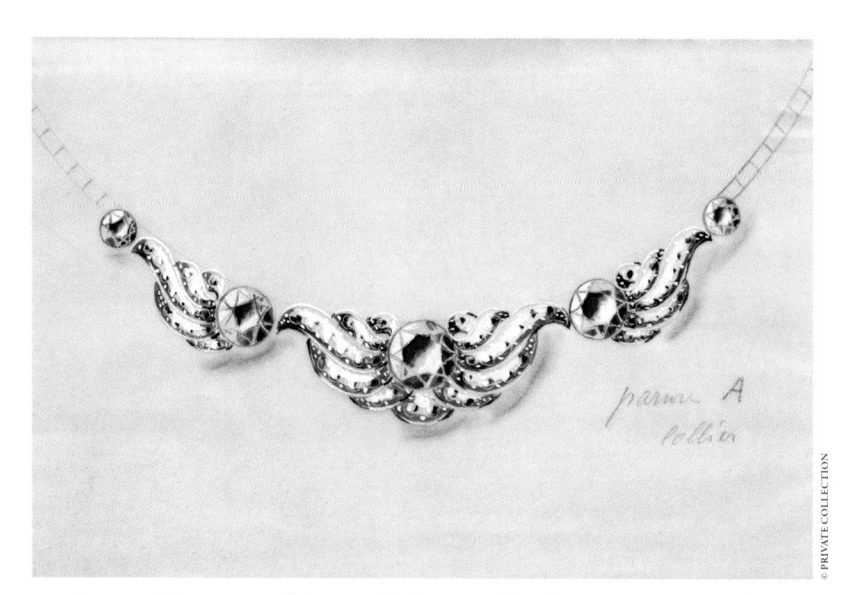

Original drawings of the jewels designed by the Lausanne jeweller, André Grumser, for Queen Sirikit on the occasion of the royal wedding

Cover of *l'Écho Illustré* dated 4 March 1950.
Departure from Lausanne for the wedding and the coronation.
The royal couple along with Magdalena Séraïdaris

Signature of the royal couple's marriage certificate

The King receives a blessing

The King bestows on his young wife the sacred royal insignia
that confer her the title of Queen

Dr Armin Däniker, representative Minister of Switzerland, and his wife

A Russian Minister and the Consul General of Switzerland

After the wedding the royal couple
greets the crowd who came to cheer

Chulalongkorn University students
pay their respects to the Queen as she passes

King Rama IX at Vadhana Villa in 1951

King Rama IX and the Queen Sirikit at Vadhana Villa in 1951

Scenes of family life of the royal couple...

...immortalized by Cléon

Travel memories immortalized by Cléon

The Queen Sirikit plays with the author,
four years old, at Vadhana Villa

12

FAREWELL LAUSANNE

During the King's extended absence while he was pursuing his studies at the Faculty of Law at the University of Lausanne, the Regency of the Kingdom was assured by his uncle, Prince Rangsit. However, the Prince's health weakened and he was unable to continue with this duty.

With the King absent there was now no Royal Family member of sufficiently high rank to assume the Regency, as the Princess Mother still resided in Switzerland, close to the King.

After consultations the King decided that, for the good of the nation, he should return to his Kingdom and take possession of his throne as his people were impatiently waiting for him. He cut short his studies in Lausanne, putting an end to his eighteen years' sojourn in Switzerland.

In making this decision the King had in mind the words of a simple and humble citizen who, after his coronation the previous year and as he was preparing to return to Switzerland, cried out "Majesty, please do not abandon us!".

Such fervour had touched him deeply. The time had come to take over the destiny of the Kingdom.

Although Princess Mahidol kept a residence in Lausanne, the Royal Family officially bade farewell to the authorities of Lausanne and of the Canton of Vaud.

13

RETURN TO THAILAND
AND BEGINNING OF REIGN

The return to Thailand, in November 1951, was once again made on the *M/S Meonia*, like the voyage in 1938. During this crossing, the King wrote frequently to his tutor.

8 November 1951

In this letter, the King started by informing his tutor of their arrival at Port Said, a technical stopover to take onboard water and supplies.

Just as during the long voyages of 1938, 1945 and 1950, the King and the Royal Family maintained a sustained and rich correspondence with Cléon, keeping him informed of their daily life, telling him of their observations about the lands they visited and their personal impressions of people and events.

In this letter written on board the *Meonia*, but posted in Colombo, the King gave an account of his numerous photographic works and the difficulties encountered in developing negatives on the ship.

There were other frustrations about the voyage. The King deplored the slow speed of the *Meonia* which could be overtaken by oil tankers. He spoke to the captain about this and the reply was, humorously, that the *Meonia* could overtake the *Queen Elizabeth*, but only if the *Meonia* passed coming in the opposite direction. He admitted that if it was true that the *Queen Elizabeth* actually sailed at 26 knots per hour, the *Meonia*, on the other hand, could only make 26 knots in two hours because her maximum speed was only 12.5 knots. The captain added, still in humorous vein that, in any event, wanting to speed up at sea would mean a loss of dignity!

The King continued to write to Cléon anecdotes which illustrated the monotonous life on board. Queen Sirikit wanted to write to Princess Mahidol who had stayed behind in Lausanne, but she was too weak from seasickness to write despite taking pills which proved ineffective.

The young Princess Ubol Ratana, the eldest daughter of the royal couple, born in April 1951 in Lausanne, had some trouble acclimatizing at first, but was well and seemingly enjoying the sea air.

The ferocious boxer dogs bought at Lausanne to stand guard in Bangkok were also seasick!

Soon after the stopover at Port Said the ship passed through the Suez Canal, heading for Singapore, without breaks for twenty days. The King remarked that during this long crossing, in case of emergency, Cléon could reach him on board by telegram, addressing it to *M/S Meonia* at the East Asiatic Company.

The King mentioned that he would send his colour films to Lausanne for developing as usual but would deal with the black and white films himself, having them enlarged in Bangkok. He finished this letter by sending greetings to Cléon and *to everybody*.

19 November 1951

In spite of everything, we stopped at Colombo to have some fresh water and fresh fruit, and it is good to break off from the constant waves and heat, His Majesty confided in this letter, actually posted in Colombo.

Then followed, as in other letters, descriptions of the landscape, observations and personal opinions on the conditions on the journey or on the members of the entourage that Cléon knows so well.

Life on the ship is perhaps monotonous, but that suit me quite well, and the King added that *it would be quite good if I had not received news that there would be a rumpus when we arrive and it would not be a restful end to the voyage.* He reassured his tutor, informing him that *whatever happens, you can be sure that I will never do anything against my will, in spite of what you may learn from the newspapers if something unusual happens.* The King obviously referred to conversations he and Cléon had had before the departure to ascend the throne.

He added: *If there are no foreign interferences it will not be serious, but if foreign nations interfere it will be a Korean war.* He asked Cléon not to inform the Princess Mother of his concern so as not to unnecessarily worry her if finally nothing happens.

The rest of the letter was again about life on board with the Queen and their young Princess, mentioning also small problems concerning their health, and told the story of his morning visit on land with the English Governor-General of Colombo.

28 November 1951

The letter was written on paper headed Bukit Serene, the High Commissioner-General's residence in Singapore. In this the King talked of a brutal awakening at 6 a.m. that morning when a 21 gun salute from the British warship greeted their arrival and escorted them into the port.

He found it really distressing that the letters and photographs promised by Cléon had not yet arrived, and took the opportunity in the breathing space between two ceremonies to write this letter. He had to make it short however to attend a meal, adding: *Departure at 3 p.m., then the boat weighs anchor at 4 p.m., accompanied for safety by a British warship until tomorrow evening, when two Siamese warships will take over [the escort] to Bangkok.*

* * *

The King's work required on arrival in the Kingdom was extensive. He had to deal with matters as diverse as the health system and modernization of communication routes. The daily life of the Thai people living in remote areas had to be improved by developing action to alleviate drought and making rational decisions about the exploitation of natural resources. Plans to end uncontrolled deforestation that accelerated erosion and brought landslides and floods in its wake were urgent. So many problems to be addressed! As for the other matters to be dealt with, the most important ones are listed in chapter 14, concerning the Royal Projects.

In 1952, the King started to use his radio broadcasting (see chapter 10) to gather the necessary funds to develop the wellbeing of the Thai. The wellbeing of his people was his major concern from the start of his reign.

The first radio broadcasts were to start the fight against poliomyelitis. The King had decided to enlarge a hospital in order to accommodate the installation of swimming pools intended for the rehabilitation of the children affected by this disease. The sovereign became personally involved in this project and called on specialized doctors to advise him on its execution.

King Bhumibol also started to travel extensively across the Kingdom to meet the Thai people of all ethnic groups. If his wish to care for them were to bear fruit he had to know their expectations, their vital needs and their living conditions. The people also had to get to know their King so he could be told of the needs of the provinces, the villages and the families. Then, having this insight the King could analyse the various situations in order to appoint executives capable of developing the Kingdom by encouraging the principle of food sufficiency, since Thailand was abundant in resources to guarantee it. Everybody should learn how to make an efficient use of these resources. King Bhumibol has been ceaseless in this work, never giving up in despite facing difficulties such as the unpredictability of the Southeast Asia's weather, sometimes struggling against the drought, sometimes against the flooding, and this tirelessly year after year.

There were not only the natural disasters in the remote provinces but also the usual flooding in the capital. The King implemented studies on how to build drainage systems and levees security that helped protecting the capital, nerve centre of the country.

The King established his main residence on the Chitralada Palace site. He added an experimental farm, included a modern dairy and cheese factory as well as research facilities dealing with agronomics, fish-farming, irrigation and other scientific issues which arose. This enabled him to keep abreast of progress and personally supervise the projects without having to waste time on travel between sites and without additional costs that would have occurred with scattered installations.

The King also set up a school nearby for the children of all the Court pages. Many years later a centre of development and production of biofuel will also be opened.

Soon after coming to the throne, the King found time to consider such details as the state of his Delahaye ceremonial motorcar bought in Paris. He found the suspension of the car unsuited to Thai roads. This car was therefore replaced by an English Daimler limousine for ceremony and a Mercedes-Benz for going up-country. The King's extensive technical knowledge and experience enabled him to choose the correct models needed to cope with the criss-cross trails found in the remote provinces while being fully capable on the streets of the capital as well.

Ever since his tender age King Bhumibol has fostered the principles of excellence in his own work and studies and he has sought to apply them to the benefit of his Kingdom. It is this application and these strengths that have enabled so many projects of such variety to be engaged upon and successfully completed for nearly sixty years.

These strict work conditions, according to a model and precepts received during his studies in Switzerland, have allowed the country to move forward and to be distinguished by training its elite in the royal universities. That is a subject of pride that all the Lausanne people could and should legitimately feel when they visit Thailand. Too few among them can remember it because they were not yet born, or maybe too young when the King studied in their city.

Daniel Brélaz, elected Mayor of Lausanne in 2001, is also a scientist. He came to understand the importance of the relationship between Lausanne and Thailand and was eager to strengthen the connections for the good of the Lausanne community. In fact he is the only Mayor of Lausanne in office to have been received on an official visit by the King in Bangkok for an audience of almost two hours. It is an honour to which Mayor Brélaz was particularly sensitive in his capacity as a mayor as well as a person.

The royal couple getting off the train before boarding on the *Meonia*

The Queen photographed by the King
during the return cruise on the *Meonia*

King Rama IX and Queen Sirikit's official arrival in the Kingdom, 2 December 1951

ALL RIGHTS RESERVED

1952, first official duties.
The King drives his Delahaye Jeep himself

The French Delahaye and the British Daimler for ceremonies

The spacious interior of the Daimler and the confined one of the Delahaye

261

The King's personal Delahaye shipped back from Lausanne

Two of the Delahaye at Klai Kang Won Palace in Hua Hin

Greeting cards crafted by Princess Mahidol,
with flowers she picked and dried herself, sent to Cléon

263

Crown Prince Maha Vajiralongkorn's birth in Bangkok, 1952. The happy grandmother holds on her lap Princess Ubolratana, the eldest daughter of the royal couple born at *Montchoisi* clinic, Lausanne

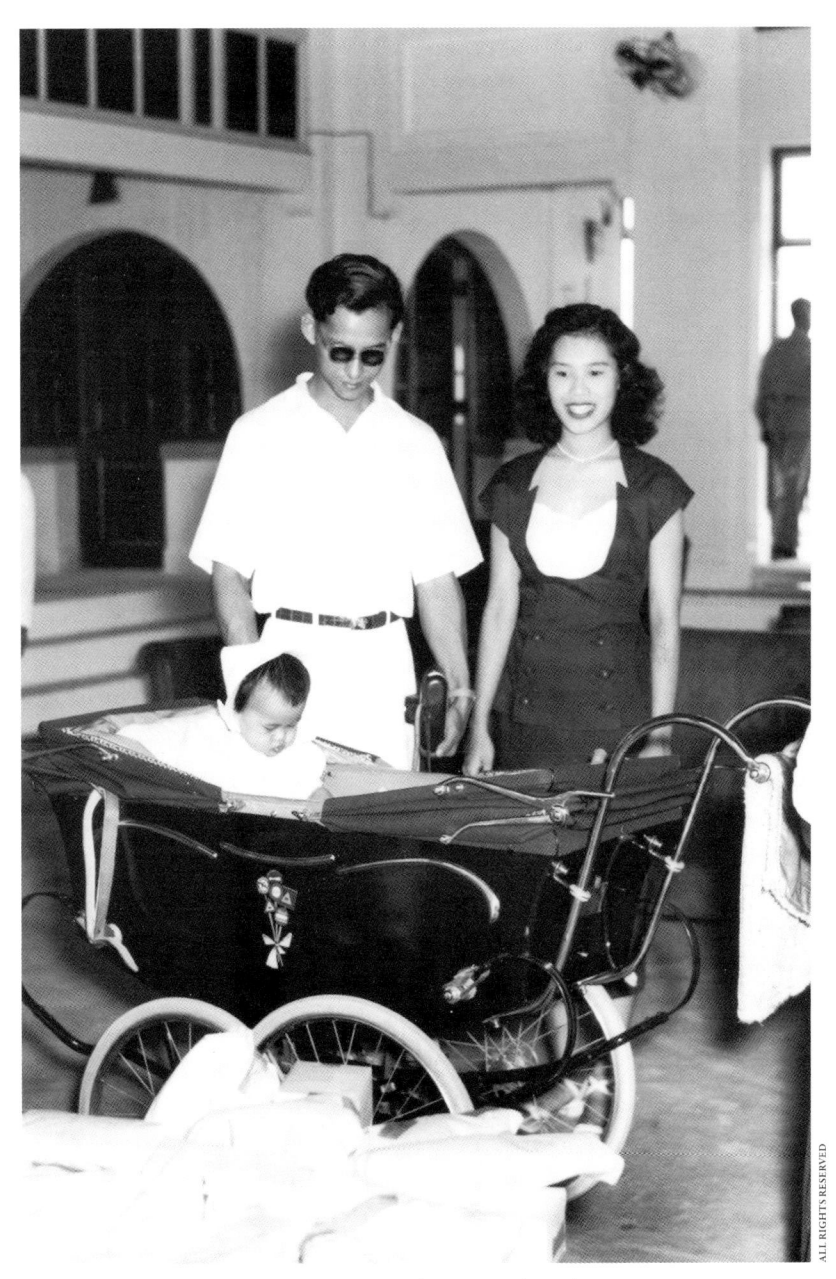

Crown Prince Maha Vajiralongkorn
in his "first car" in Bangkok in 1952

The Royal Family in Bangkok, 11 November 1956

Princess Mahidol, 1 January 1957

The Royal Family in 1960

14

THE ROYAL PROJECTS, MASTERPIECES OF THE KING

Thailand being a constitutional monarchy, the King has no overt political role. He acts in order to serve his Kingdom by means of his philanthropic foundations where, through the Royal Projects, development of the structure of the nation and the welfare of its peoples, regardless of origin, class or religion are served. These works earn him a great respect and an absolute gratitude, almost a feeling of veneration, from the Thai people.

Having seen the success of Thailand in the globalization at the end of the 20th century, one understands that the King succeeded in taking up the challenge. The saying is that Rome was not built in one day, but the facts show us that since the King came back from his studies in Switzerland, Thailand has modernized and has adapted in time to take its place in the 21st century as a leading Asian nation.

The implementation of these various and important works earned the King a number of scientific awards from renowned institutions, including the prestigious Massachusetts Institute of Technology (MIT).

The Royal Projects represent works undertaken to develop agriculture, fish-farming, traditional craft, industry, urban planning, and everything that help to modernize the country, make it competitive, and especially make it independent in all possible fields within the principle of self-sufficiency.

During nearly sixty years, King Bhumibol has personally initiated and supervised over three thousand projects, all of them important for the future of the Kingdom and of its people. As an example, one of the King's decisions, drawn from his experience in Canton of Vaud, was the distribution of milk in schools, for which he had great admiration. At the beginning of the 1950s, school children of various communes of the Canton of Vaud received each week a small bottle of warm milk in class.

The King has always been fond of daily fresh milk, even when he became an adult. He decided to do everything so that milk was distributed to the Thai school children, to enhance their growth. However, the King recognized that to fulfil this aspiration not only would dairy farming need improvement but that milk production and distribution capacity would be necessary. Thailand did not have a dairy industry able to produce sufficient daily quantity of fresh milk to realize this ambition.

The project, named School Milk Program, began in 1960, during an official visit to Denmark and was fulfilled after twenty-five years of assiduous work, with the support of King Frederick IX of Denmark, who contributed financially from its inception.

In 1985, the National Youth Office, depending on the Prime Minister's Office, was put in charge of organizing this distribution of milk in schools.

Due to his training acquired from the State of Fribourg Agricultural Institute, HE Lord Chamberlain Kaewkhwan Vajarodaya was appointed to be responsible for the agricultural projects of the King.

At the same time, as mentioned in chapter 13, an experimental farm was built on the Chitralada Palace site, the new official residence of the sovereign, so that he could oversee the works. It is at this place that the milk from the School Milk Program is packed in aseptic cartons using Tetra Pak UHT (ultra-high temperature) process, at the rate of 7,500 cartons of 200 ml per hour. There, one also finds a cheese factory, workshops producing ice-cream and condensed milk pastilles to suck, plain or cocoa, very pleasant and much healthier than sweets or other candies that are not recommended for children's teeth.

Other Royal Projects, too many to list here, are concerned with the following, these being enacted in and around the capital city and out in the rural areas.

Primary Development Projects are:
- Education of rural population
- Rural zones
- Agriculture
- Rice bank

- Fish-farming
- Rearing of buffaloes and cattle
- Traditional craft

Other projects were initiated in the following fields:
- Protection of water resources
- Protection of forests
- Artificial rain inducement in drought areas
- Creation of mobile medical units
- Construction of unloading tanks to solve recurring problems of flooding in Bangkok and in its suburbs

An important education project:

The King founded the Klai Kang Won School at Hua Hin, where he has taught students personally. As part of his distant learning project, he has also made available, at this school, classes whose recorded courses are broadcast twenty-four hours daily via the Internet.

HE Khun Khwankeo Vajarodaya; Lysandre C. Séraïdaris;
Mr Daniel Brélaz, Lausanne Mayor; HE Dr Chaiyong Satjipanon,
Ambassador of Thailand in Bern; and Dr Rosesarin Smitabhindu
on Chitralada site, in front of the milk packing machine of the School
Milk Program during Mr Brélaz's visit in 2008

HE Khun Khwankeo Vajarodaya invites Mayor Daniel Brélaz
to test the production of dairy products

Visit of the rice mill sector on Chitralada site

Tetra Pak eco-friendly cardboard packs conditioned and packed on Chitralada site, within the School Milk Program

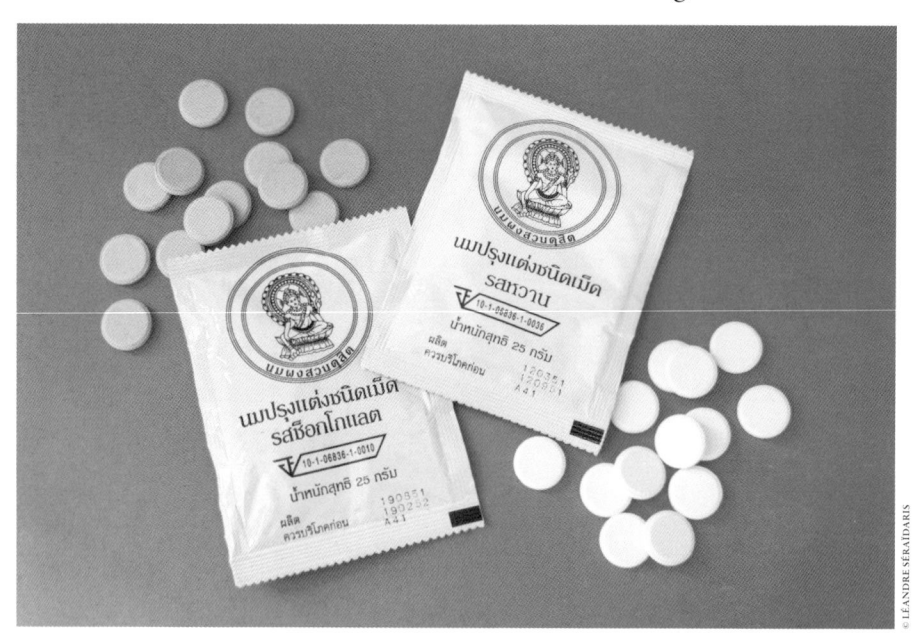

Lozenges of the School Milk Program produced on Chitralada site

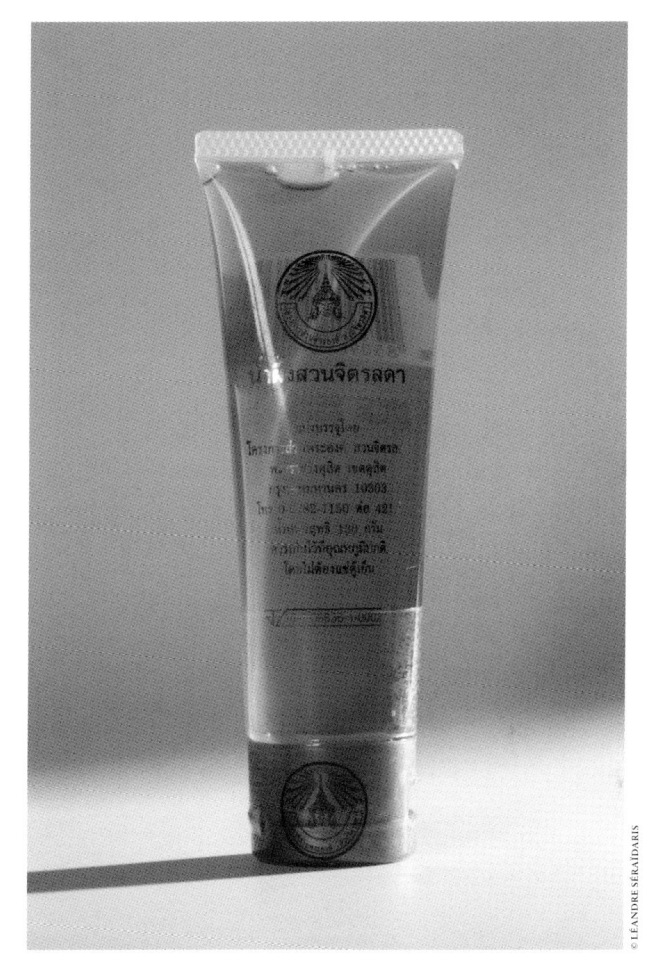

Honey produced as part of the Royal Projects

HE Khun Khwankeo Vajarodaya; Lysandre C. Séraïdaris;
Mr Daniel Brélaz, Lausanne Mayor; HE Dr Chaiyong Satjipanon,
Ambassador of Thailand in Bern on the site...

... of the Foundation for Distance Learning, in a French class at Klai Kang Won School, Hua Hin, during Mr Brélaz's visit in 2008

Toast to the success of the relationship between Lausanne and Thailand

The author, Mr Daniel Brélaz et HE Khun Khwankeo Vajarodaya with students at Klai Kang Won School

15

DIPLOMATIC VISITS AND LEISURE STAY

In 1960, His Majesty King Bhumibol returned to Europe on an official trip, visiting European Heads of State. The King wished to set up his Headquarters at Lausanne or in the vicinity. This would enable him to reach the various European capitals while the Royal children could enjoy getting acquainted with the region that their parents were so fond of.

The Royal Thai Embassy in Bern looked for a sufficiently large and comfortable residence offering the necessary security to accommodate the Royal Family. Flonzaley, the family home of lawyer Jean-René Mermoud, and his father before him, became available and was seen as ideal.

Flonzaley is an exceptional property, located directly above the village of Epesses, having a panoramic view over Lake Léman.

During this extended stay trips to European capitals were interspersed with official visits in Switzerland and leisure excursions. The King was able to have his children discover the countryside with pedal boats on Lake Léman, walks at Ouchy and across French-speaking Switzerland and winter sports.

The author remembers football matches played on the lawn at Flonzaley with the Crown Prince Maha Vajiralongkorn, where the Canton of Vaud Security Police officers sometimes took part.

Other times His Majesty worked with his tutor, his private secretaries and aides-de-camp on preparations for official visits, and then went out into the garden to join in the games. Later came tea for everyone, with the traditional glass of fresh milk, including one for the King.

During the grape harvest the King visited the vineyards. The vintners were delighted and huge baskets of superb grapes were delivered to Flonzaley. Coincidentally, a member of one of the Epesses wine-producing family, Ambassador Gérard Fonjallaz, later became Switzerland's Representative in Bangkok.

When winter came, the King wanted his children to experience and enjoy ice-skating and skiing, the latter being one of his favourite sports. For the New Year celebrations, a reservation was made in Gstaad at the Palace Hotel, the best in the region. The Royal Family spent a memorable time there thanks to the attentive hoteliers, the Scherz family. Naturally, as in the past, Cléon was by the King's side during this festive period.

That year, New Year's Eve was unforgettable. No less than "Satchmo", the great Louis Armstrong in person entertained the Royal Family. He had crossed the Atlantic on the occasion and was delighted to perform for them. The Scherz were equally honoured to welcome to their hotel both the King and the famous jazzman who knew each other well.

The following morning the King and Cléon, both excellent skiers, began giving the Queen her first skiing lesson. A learning experience and hard work... but filled with laughter and good humour.

Once back at Flonzaley, the tutor would accompany the King on strictly private engagements, just as in times past. A few weeks without official visits abroad also allowed the King to take his children to Gstaad and to the *Montchoisi* skating rink where the author joined them as soon as he had finished his classes at *Champittet* College next to the rink. The Crown Prince started learning ice hockey with the King and tutor, the latter having also taught it to the King at Davos more than twenty years earlier. In the meantime, Princess Ubol Ratana practiced skating with the author, who was also eager to pass on the basics to the young Princess Maha Chakri Sirindhorn who progressed quickly. Both the Princess Maha Chakri Sirindhorn and the author still retain happy memories of those days on the ice. As for the little Princess Chulabhorn Walailak, who courageously followed the example of her elders, discovering the joy of snow and ice sports.

After these long months spent in Europe, the Royal Family returned to Bangkok.

***

The King returned to Switzerland for a last stay of about two weeks in autumn 1964, this time staying at the Hotel *Beau-Rivage Palace* in Lausanne, well-renowned for having welcomed Heads of State and international conferences, as it was not necessary to rent a residence for such a short period. The royal couple consented to sign the Hotel's precious Visitors Book.

At a sports day organized on a Sunday, the King played badminton in a hall of the *Palais de Beaulieu* at Lausanne with his entourage, the tutor and the latter's son. Badminton was also a sport at which the King excelled and he imposed on his Lausanne partners a vigorous rhythm.

This was the last visit of the King of Thailand to the City of Lausanne, as a few years later, King Bhumibol decided to devote himself entirely to the internal good and development of the Kingdom and never again to leave it, judging that the important works of modernization and development were his first priority. He delegated the responsibility of representing him overseas to his sister Princess Galyani Vadhana and to other high ranking members of the Royal Family.

* * *

Princess Mahidol continued her visits to Switzerland regularly, mainly to Lausanne and the mountains. The change of climate benefited her health. She met many of her friends who could not travel to Thailand. This also allowed her to take a break from the official duties, often stressful, that she had to assure in the Kingdom.

The Princess, who in later life was affectionately known in Thailand as the "Grandmother of the Kingdom", kept up with engagements of humanitarian acts in the provinces, visiting the monastic community and sponsoring projects to assist women and children. Her work reached out to help orphanages and hospitals of the islands, the rural areas and the mountainous regions, mostly very far from the urban centres. That was why the people regarded Princess Mahidol with limitless admiration and deep respect.

Arrival of the royal couple at Geneva airport, along with Cléon, and welcomed by the Geneva authorities

Stirring welcome for the royal couple in Chexbres

Welcoming of Mr Paul Chaudet, President of the Swiss Confederation

The King reviews a detachment of the police force
of Canton of Vaud in parade uniform

The royal couple in Bern with Mr Max Petitpierre,
new President of the Swiss Confederation

The Royal Family on the terrace of Flonzaley Villa

HM Queen Sirikit on Flonzaley Villa stairs

Princess Ubol Ratana with her parents
in the Flonzaley property

Royal children playing in the garden of Flonzaley Villa

Walk through the Flonzaley property.
Princess Maha Chakri Sirindhorn offers flowers she had picked

On the quay in Ouchy.
The Royal Family returns from a pedal boat ride on Lake Léman

Crown Prince Maha Vajiralongkorn and Princess Ubol Ratana
with the author in the garden of Flonzaley Villa

A Louis Armstrong concert at the Palace Hotel in Gstaad

Hockey lesson by the King and the tutor

HM Queen Sirikit and Cléon at Gstaad

The King and Cléon, experienced skiers,
give the Queen her first ski lesson

Little Princess Chulabhorn Walailak
also started skiing at that time

Princess Mahidol was an experienced skier

Montchoisi skating rink, Lausanne.
Princess Ubol Ratana follows the author's advice

The author explains also to the young and attentive
Princess Maha Chakri Sirindhorn how to keep balance on ice

A walk in the Alps where Princess Mahidol
liked regularly to come and rest

Princess Mahidol picked flowers in the pasture.
She dried them to adorn her greeting cards

Princess Mahidol with Rasmi and Marcelle Suriyong,
their son Surin, Cléon, and an unidentified friend

HRH Princess Mahidol insisted on preparing the meal

Princesses Mahidol and Galyani at the miniature golf
with Cléon in Lausanne

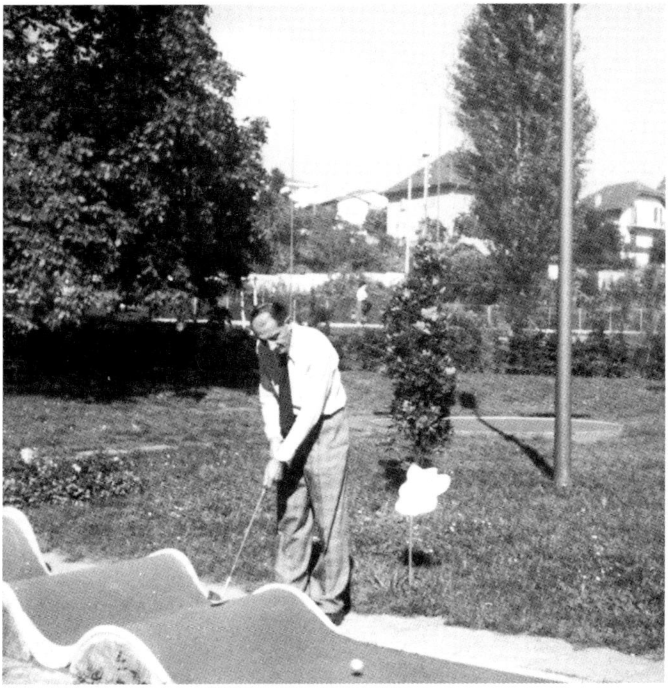

© PRIVATE COLLECTION

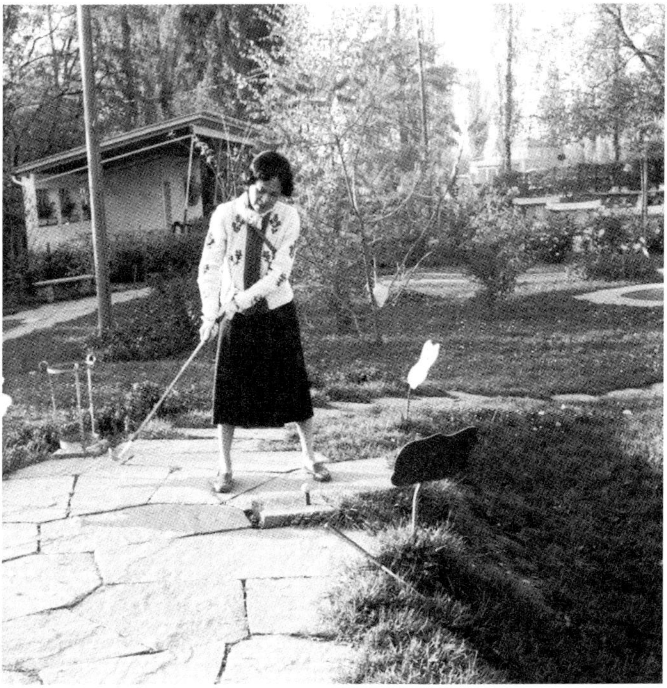

© PRIVATE COLLECTION

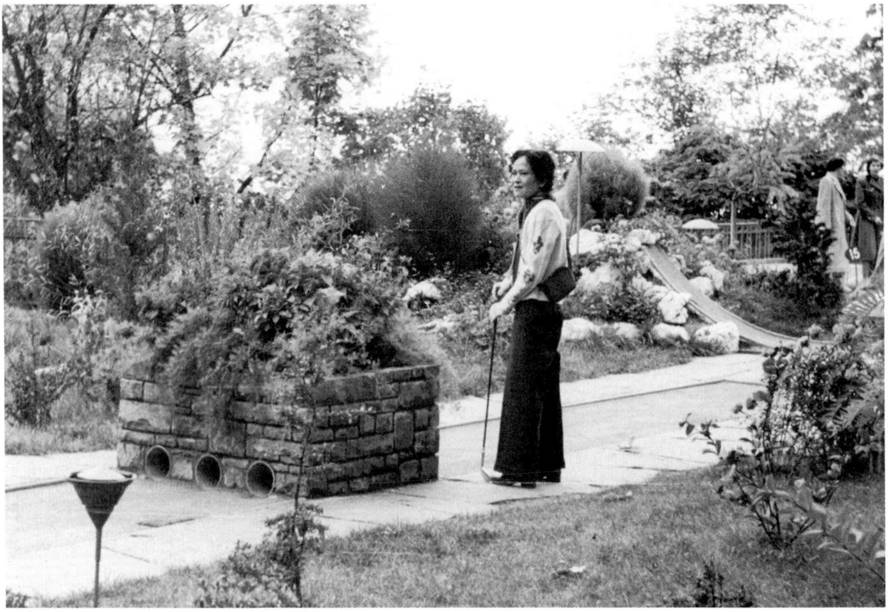

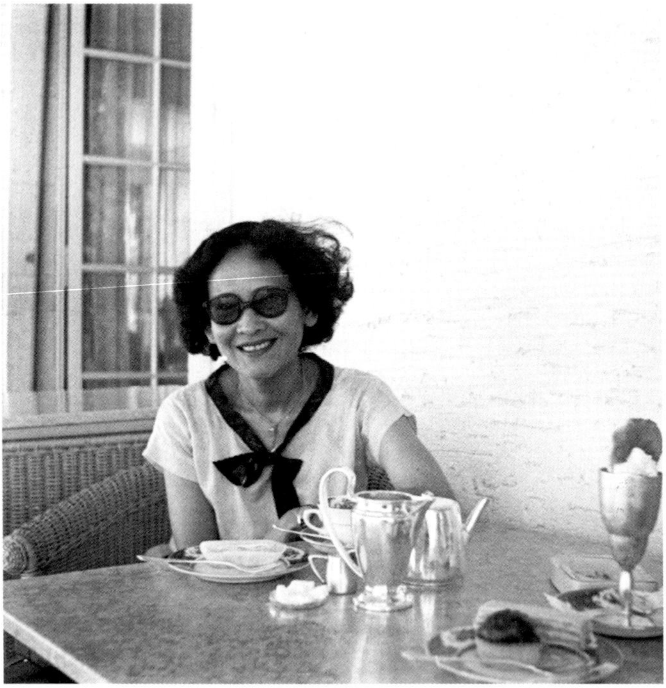

Princess Mahidol looking for beautiful flowers to dry
in the forest near Lausanne

Princess Mahidol on the balcony of her residence,
Avenue de l'Avant-Poste, Lausanne

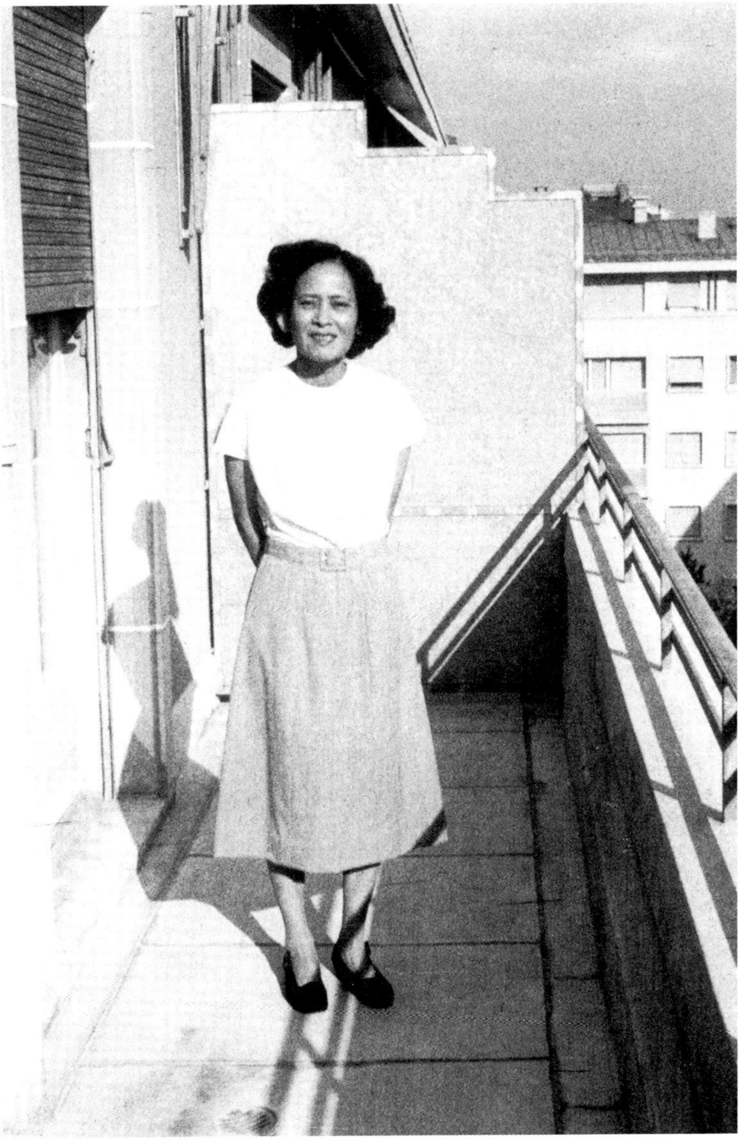

© PRIVATE COLLECTION

This interlude brought him much gratification and he was happy to pass on to the young man the precepts that Mr Rusconi and his wife immensely appreciated. Did Jean-Baptiste realize at the time that he benefited from the kindly advice of the private tutor of His Majesty the King of Thailand?

However, the most important of Cléon's occupations during retirement was to take care of his wife Magdalena who suffered from rheumatoid arthritis and needed daily attention until her death in January 1980.

* * *

There was also a special place in Cléon's memory for the welcome and magnificent stay the King offered him in Thailand with his son Lysandre and the latter's family. He was then eighty-two years of age.

Apart from emotional reunions at private audiences with the King and in the company of the Queen and of Princess Maha Chakri Sirindhorn, he also had the opportunity of spending long hours with Princess Mahidol, at Bhubing Palace in Chiang Mai, as well as in Bangkok with Princess Galyani Vadhana, in her *Le Dix* residence at Sukhumvit 43.

Despite his old age Cléon managed to visit historic sites, residences and royal palaces as well as the Royal Projects and the craft centres. There were delightful evening engagements where dinners were held in his honour, alternating with cultural and entertainment events.

There was even a traditional boat trip along the Chao Phraya River to the sea, escorted by two Royal Thai river patrol boats in order to cope with any unforeseen events at the approach to deep waters. To make this long tour pleasurable, there were many cooks who prepared exceptional dishes for His Majesty's guests. The trip was a source of amazement for the young Alexandra, Cléon's granddaughter who accompanied him during the whole stay.

The Grand Chamberlain HE Khun Khwankeo Vajarodaya, Head of the Royal Household, took particular care by accompanying the tutor and in arranging his escort.

His Majesty King Rama IX
receives the tutor and his family for an audience in 1988

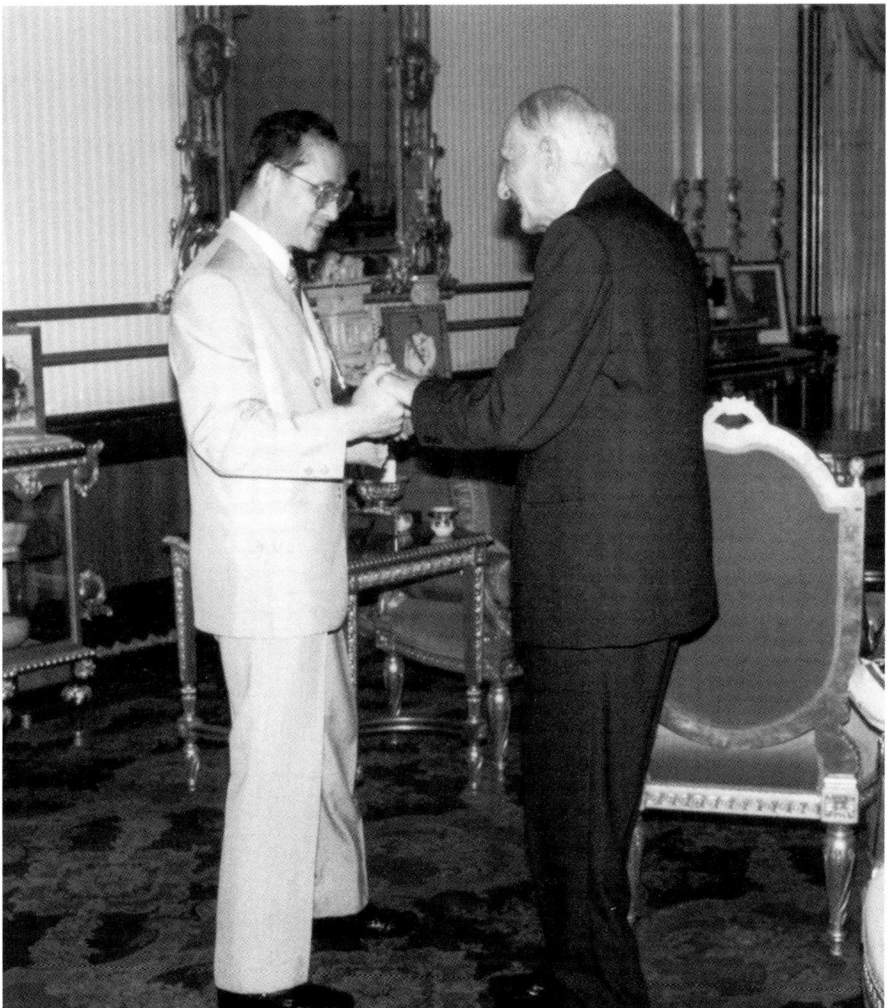

© PRIVATE COLLECTION

King Rama IX is surrounded by the tutor and his family:
the author, Mrs Catherine Séraïdaris and young Alexandra Séraïdaris

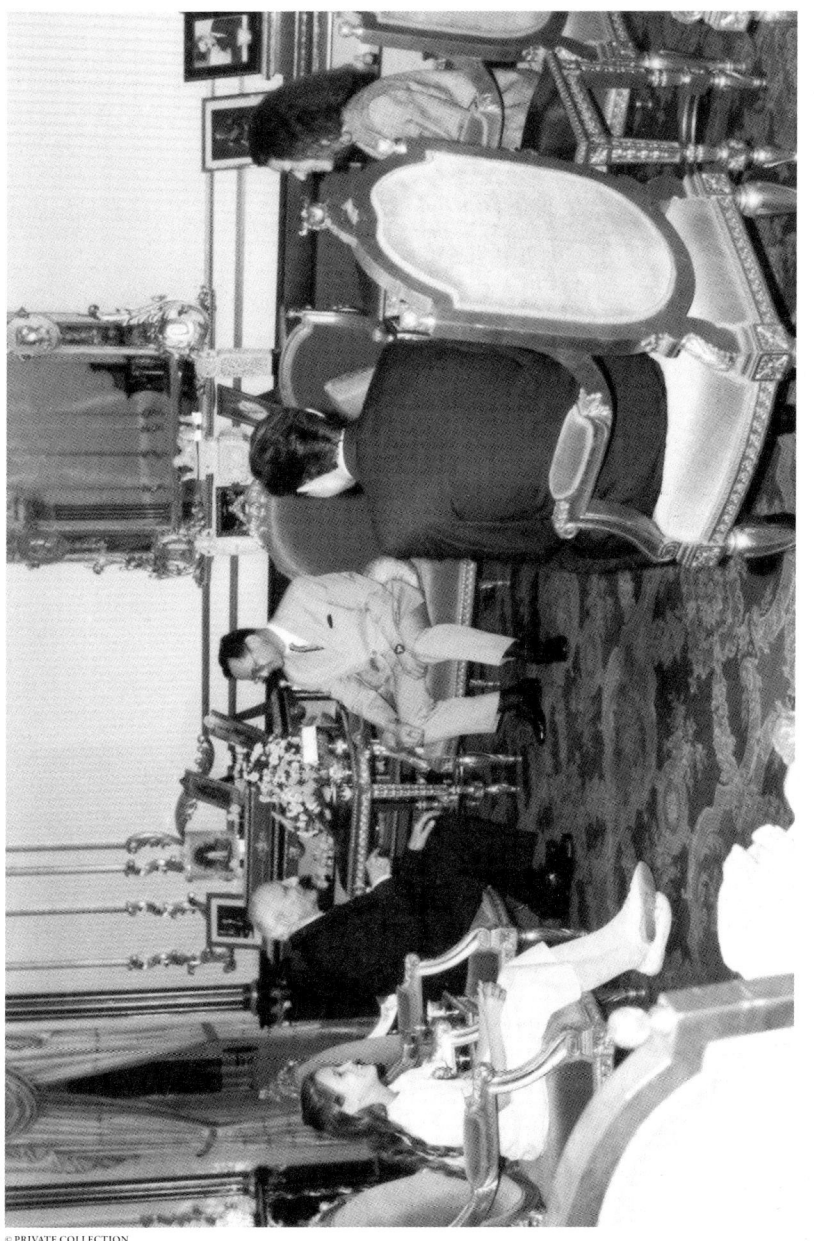

© PRIVATE COLLECTION

Cléon congratulates HM the King on his interpretation on the trumpet of one of his compositions

The King receives with great interest a book that Cléon brought him from Switzerland

The King handing some books to Cléon in memory of his trip to Bangkok, during a private audience which he granted him at the Chitralada Palace

Princess Maha Chakri Sirindhorn wishes Cléon and his family
a pleasant return trip to Switzerland

Cléon and his family admiring roses in the garden of Bhubing Palace
in Chiang Mai with HE Khun Khwankeo Vajarodaya

Cléon at the Monastery of Bang Pa In Palace in Ayutthaya

HE Khun Khwankeo Vajarodaya, the author, Cléon
and Alexandra Séraïdaris in Bang Pa In

HE Khun Khwankeo Vajarodaya and Thanpuying Wattana Vajarodaya were keen to show the elephants to Cléon and his family

Cléon and his granddaughter on the Chao Phraya River

Souvenir photo of the traditional boat trip
along the Chao Phraya River

Cléon and Thanpuying Wattana Vajarodaya

HE Khun Khwankeo Vajarodaya, Catherine, Lysandre,
Alexandra et Cléon Séraïdaris

Stopover to visit traditional craft workshops

Cléon, who knows a lot about woodworking, watching how to use a traditional tool, with his granddaughter Alexandra and Thanpuying Wattana Vajarodaya

17

A GREAT LADY LEAVES LAUSANNE

On 21 October 1990, Princess Mahidol gave a large reception at the Grand Hall of Pully, in celebration of her ninetieth birthday gathering the Thai community at Lausanne. This event, whose the oldest members of the community still remember perfectly today, was of importance for it was held in Pully, residence of the Royal Family until early 1952, then a secondary residence of Princess Galyani Vadhana from the 1950s.

Indeed Princess Galyani Vadhana first lived at *Boulevard de la Forêt* and then later at *Avenue de Lavaux* in Pully, where Princess Mahidol came to join her in the 1980s as it was not appropriate for her to stay by herself at *Avenue de l'Avant-Poste* in Lausanne.

This celebration at Pully was a more important event than just a birthday. A ninetieth birthday is in itself a notable event but it was about an exceptional person of whom all the Thais thought of as their Grandmother.

But above all it was actually Princess Mahidol's farewell to the Pully region and to Lausanne since, a few weeks later, this Great Lady left Switzerland for good. Her eyesight had declined and her health had progressively deteriorated over the years, and the King did not want to be far from his mother in case she had health problems.

When one realizes how much Switzerland meant to her (she had lived there some of the happiest years together with her three children), one could understand that for her it was an important page turned. The Princess used to come to Switzerland every year, especially to Lausanne, and also to the Bernese Oberland, despite the important duties she assured in Thailand where the people called her the "Grandmother of the Kingdom" due to her wisdom and her lifelong devotion to charitable work with underprivileged families.

The departure from this region was certainly another trial for this great friend of Switzerland. However, at this reception Princess Mahidol showed no sadness, only great joy in being at this celebration surrounded by the entire community.

Later, while supervising the construction projects of Buddhist temples in the North of Thailand and in German-speaking Switzerland, the Princess became again an attentive mother who first concern was her illustrious son's health. The King regularly went to his mother's residence to have lunch as she wanted to cook herself his favourite dishes that he was fond of, like all the mothers in the world.

On 18 July 1995, HRH Princess Mahidol Srinagarindra died peacefully, three months before her ninety-fifth birthday.

Cléon, to his great distress, was unable to attend the funeral as his state of health prevented him from travelling. He had to be hospitalized in the autumn of 1995, and then watched over at home day and night until the end of his life in April 1997.

Princess Mahidol at her ninetieth birthday celebration,
along with Princess Galyani Vadhana and Cléon

Princess Mahidol receives wishes from Cléon,
Lysandre and Alexandra Séraïdaris

Princess Mahidol and Princess Galyani Vadhana receive Cléon and the author in their Pully residence

18

THE TUTOR'S LAST MOMENTS

The King's tutor lived in Lausanne for eighty-one years and died at an advanced age on 9 April 1997, three months before his ninety-first birthday.

It happened that HRH Princess Maha Chakri Sirindhorn was on a private visit to Switzerland that day. The author spent most of the afternoon in her company, in Flonzaley, at the home of the lawyer Jean-René Mermoud, who had invited the Princess to see once again the house where she had spent almost a year of her childhood, when Their Majesties the King and Queen returned to Europe.

The Thai Ambassador in Bern, HE Don Pramudwinai alerted the Princess that Cléon, her father's tutor, had become very weak over several days past and was bedridden. The Princess may think it opportune to visit Cléon soon. Sensitive to this homage, the author, the tutor's youngest son, told the Ambassador that he would go immediately to his father's bedside to decide with the nurse on duty there the most appropriate time for the Princess's visit to Cléon the following day.

Arriving home he saw that his father was asleep, watched over by his grandson, Léandre. They decided not to wake him up but let him rest some before speaking to him. Soon after, Léandre found Cléon was having breathing difficulties and he alerted the nurse. Nothing could be done. The King's tutor quietly passed away in his grandson's arms.

Princess Sirindhorn's visit to her father's tutor could unfortunately not take place. The King was immediately informed and he charged, as is formal protocol, the Grand Chamberlain to telephone the author and give the King's personal expressions of sympathy and grief that His Majesty felt for his tutor's sons.

Cléon Séraïdaris funeral was conducted according to the rites of the Greek Orthodox Church in Lausanne attended by hundreds of mourners. After his family the principle person attending was the Thai Ambassador in Bern, by command of His Majesty King Bhumibol. The funeral cortege was escorted by the Lausanne City Police to accompany to his final resting place the tutor, who had been the keystone of the two Kings' studies and who had worked to consolidate the attachment of the Royal Family to the City of Lausanne.

Cléon Séraïdaris was buried at the *Bois-de-Vaux* Cemetery in Lausanne, on 14 April 1997. He is on the list of personalities resting in this cemetery, the largest one in the region.

Last photograph of Cléon C. Séraïdaris
with his son, the author, in autumn 1996

École Nouvelle de la Suisse Romande

Association of Alumni

                              Mr Lysandre Séraïdaris
                              and family

                              14 April 1997

Dear Sir,

It is with great sorrow that we learned of the death of Mr Cléon Seraïdaris, loyal member of our Association, former pupil and teacher at the École Nouvelle.

He was one of the veterans of our school and we are proud to have had the honour to count him among our members. His role as tutor to the King of Thailand has greatly contributed to the reputation of our school in Switzerland and worldwide. For us, his passing represents the loss of a great friend of the École Nouvelle.

Please accept my most sincere condolences at this sad time.

Yours sincerely,

                              Edmond de Braun,
                              President

                Translation of the document of the right page

ECOLE NOUVELLE DE LA SUISSE ROMANDE
Fondée en 1906

ASSOCIATION DES ANCIENS
20 ch. de Rovéréaz
CH -1012 LAUSANNE
CCP 10 - 9825-8

Monsieur Lysandre C. Séraïdaris
et famille
Chemin de Verdeil 22

1005 Lausanne

le 14 avril 1997

Monsieur,

C'est avec grande tristesse que nous avons pris connaissance de l'annonce du décès de Monsieur Cléon Séraïdaris, fidèle membre de notre association, ancien élève et professeur de l'Ecole Nouvelle.

Il faisait partie de ses Anciens dont on peut s'enorgueillir d'avoir eu l'honneur de le compter parmi nos membres. Son rôle de précepteur du Roi de Thaïlande a très largement contribué au rayonnement de notre Ecole en Suisse et dans le monde. Son départ représente donc pour nous celui d'un très grand ami de l'Ecole Nouvelle.

Nous vous présentons en cette triste occasion nos plus sincères condoléances.

Veuillez agréer, Monsieur, nos salutations distinguées.

Edmond de Braun
président

Letter of condolence from the President of the Association of Alumni of *École Nouvelle de la Suisse Romande* following the tutor's death

The tutor's grave with flowers from the Royal Family

19

HRH PRINCESS GALYANI VADHANA

Princess Galyani, elder sister of the two Kings, was born on 6 May 1923 in London where her parents Prince Mahidol of Songkla and his young wife, Princess Sangwal Mahidol Srinagarindra were staying. Her given birth name was May, but her uncle, King Vajiravudh (Rama VI) soon conferred on her the style and title of Mom Chao Galyani Vadhana, that is to say Her Serene Highness Galyani Vadhana.

Her education in Switzerland was different from that of her two brothers. She attended the *Champ Soleil* Primary School, then the *Miremont* School with them, but she then registered at the Lausanne High School for Girls. Princess Galyani did not have a private tutor and continued her studies at the International School of Geneva where she distinguished herself at the baccalaureate. She obtained first place at the school and third place at national level. Then at the University of Lausanne she followed courses at the Faculty of Pharmacy and in parallel courses in French literature, philosophy and psychology.

Princess Galyani had interest in skiing, mountain-hiking, horseback-riding, badminton (she often went to the Badminton Club in Lausanne with her mother and Cléon), miniature golf, motoring and even piloting aeroplanes.

In 1944, Princess Galyani married Khun Aram Ratanakul, Colonel in the Thai Army. This resulted in her temporarily losing her title because her husband was not of royal descent. The couple lived in the Lausanne region. Their daughter Dhasanawalaya was born in 1945.

In 1950, a Royal Decree restored her title as HRH Princess Galyani Vadhana. Returning to Thailand that same year she attended the funeral rites of King Ananda, her brother, who had died tragically in 1946.

Since the official return of the Royal Family to Thailand at the end of 1951, Princess Galyani alternately stayed in Switzerland, where she had kept a residence and in Bangkok where she became a part-time teacher of French language, literature and civilization at Chulalongkorn University, one of Thailand's most prestigious universities.

In 1969 she accepted a full-time post at Thammasat University where she spent seven years as Head of French language and literature Department. She was then made Professor *Emeritus* at Thammasat while being visiting Professor at the Universities of Chiang Mai and Kasetsart and at Prince of Songkla University in Pattani.

Princess Galyani Vadhana worked tirelessly for the nation. In addition to her own work and responsibilities, she joined her mother, Princess Mahidol Srinagarindra, in improving education. They travelled throughout the land, to the remote areas, the mountainous regions and the islands, going places where their presence would encourage children at school. Teaching materials donated by Royal Foundations were provided.

On 6 May 1995, on the occasion of her sixth cycle, that is to say her seventy-second birthday, His Majesty the King conferred upon her the highest title of nobility for a Princess: Krom Luang. She thus became "Princess Galyani Vadhana Krom Luang Naradhiwas Rajanagarindra" just before the death of the Princess Mother on 18 July 1995.

Passionate about classical music, Princess Galyani attended the International Festival of Classical Music at Verbier in Switzerland every year. She set up a fund for the promotion of classical music in Thailand with the aim of facilitating young Thai musicians to study in European countries. Princess Galyani acted as President of this fund.

Although her daughter, Thanpuying Dhasanawalaya, insisted that her mother should slow down her activity level and even suggested a full year's rest, Princess Galyani, despite being in her eighties, continued to work unremittingly, accompanying the medical teams out to the remotest regions and taking under her protection sick people whom she then sent on to appropriate hospitals. This willingness to give practical hands-on help the delegated the author to represent the City of Lausanne and its people at the grandiose funeral ceremony of Princess Galyani Vadhana.

On a personal note, the author was particularly honoured to be invited to attend the private royal cremation ceremony of the late Princess Galyani Vadhana.

The King and Princess Galyani Vadhana at Flonzaley Villa in 1960

Princess Galyani Vadhana and her daughter Dhasanawalaya
around 1950

Princess Galyani and Princess Mahidol
at the *Avenue de l'Avant-Poste* résidence, autumn 1958

Princess Galyani, her grandson Khun Jitat Sornsongkram,
in his great-grandmother Princess Mahidol's arms, and Dhasanawalaya

Princess Galyani with her daughter Thanpuying Dhasanawalaya
and her grandson Khun Jitat Sornsongkram

Princess Galyani Vadhana accompanying Cléon and his family during a visit at Wat Po and Wat Phra Keo

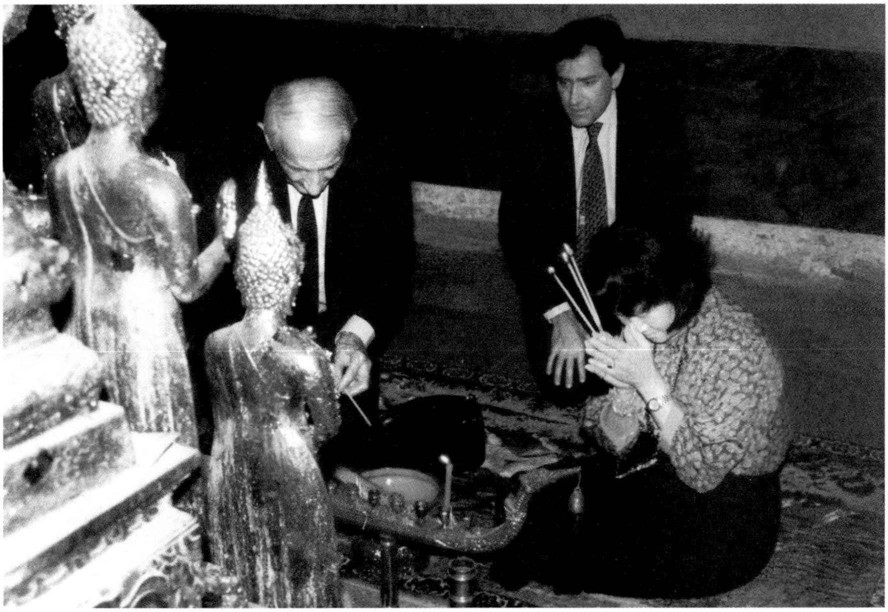

© PRIVATE COLLECTION

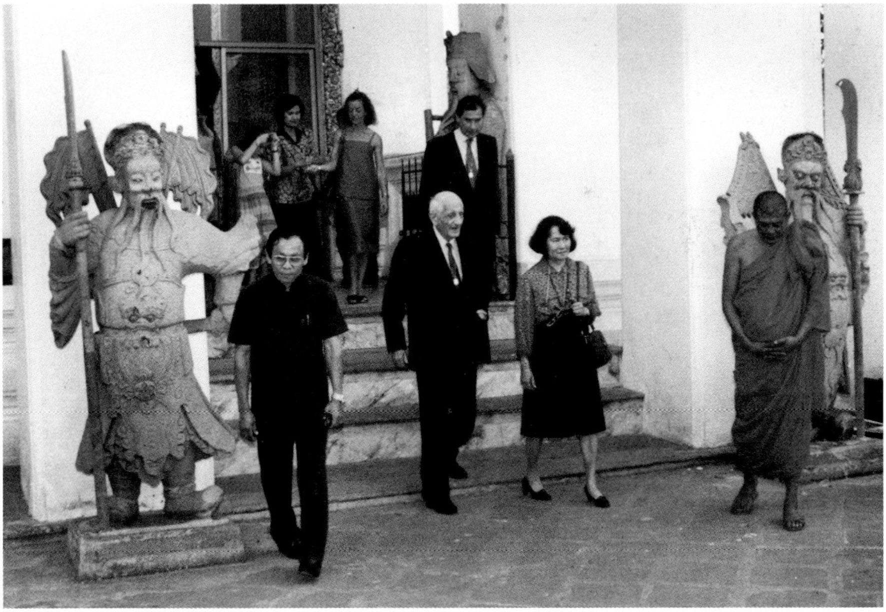

© PRIVATE COLLECTION

(City of Lausanne)
General Administration and Finance

The Mayor

                                        His Majesty the King of Thailand
                                        Bangkok
                                        Kingdom of Thailand

                                        Lausanne, 7 January 2008

Your Majesty,

The authorities and the people of Lausanne were extremely saddened to hear the news of the death of Her Royal Highness Princess Galyani Vadhana.

We would like to offer Your Majesty our heartfelt condolences and our respectful and deepest sympathy for the loss of such an illustrious lady who was at heart a Lausannoise and who lived in our city for such a long time and was respected and appreciated by all our fellow citizens who had the honour of knowing her.

On behalf of the authorities and the people of Lausanne, please accept, Your Majesty, the assurance of my highest esteem.

                                                        Daniel Brélaz
                                                    Mayor of Lausanne

             Translation of the document of the right page

administration générale et
finances

le syndic

Sa Majesté le Roi de Thaïlande
Bangkok
Royaume de Thaïlande

DB/gp

Lausanne, le 7 janvier 2008

Majesté,

Les Autorités et la population de Lausanne ont été particulièrement peinées d'apprendre la triste nouvelle du décès de Son Altesse Royale la Princesse Galyani Vadhana.

Nous aimerions présenter à Votre Majesté nos plus sincères condoléances et nos sentiments de respectueuse et profonde sympathie pour la disparition d'une illustre Lausannoise de cœur, qui a si longtemps résidé dans notre cité et qui était respectée et appréciée par tous nos concitoyens qui ont eu l'honneur de la connaître.

Au nom des Autorités et de la population de Lausanne, je prie Votre Majesté d'agréer l'assurance de ma très haute considération.

Daniel Brélaz
Syndic de Lausanne

Hôtel de Ville
place de la Palud 2
case postale 6904
CH-1002 Lausanne
tél. 4121 315 22 00

Letter of condolence from Lausanne authorities
signed by Mr Daniel Brélaz, Lausanne Mayor

City of Pully
Municipality

His Majesty the King of Thailand
Bangkok
Kingdom of Thailand

Pully, 9 January 2008

Your Majesty,

It is with sadness that we learned of the death of Her Royal Highness Princess Galyani Vadhana.

The authorities of the City of Pully beg Your Majesty to accept their most sincere condolences.

The death of Princess Galyani Vadhana represents an irreplaceable loss for the Kingdom of Thailand. The people of Pully retain fond memories of this distinguished Pully resident whom they knew and lived alongside for many years.

On behalf of the Municipality
The Vice-President   The Secretary
Maria-Chrystina Cuendet   *Corinne Martin*

Translation of the document of the right page

ville de pully
Municipalité

Sa Majesté le Roi de Thaïlande
Bangkok
Royaume de Thaïlande

Pully, le 9 janvier 2008

Majesté,

C'est avec tristesse que nous avons appris le décès de Son Altesse Royale la Princesse Galyani Vadhana.

Les Autorités de la Ville de Pully prient votre Majesté de bien vouloir accepter leurs condoléances les plus sincères.

La disparition irremplaçable de la Princesse Galyani Vadhana pour le Royaume de Thaïlande laissera un souvenir ému aux Pulliérans qui ont connu et côtoyé cette illustre résidente de Pully depuis de si longues années.

AU NOM DE LA MUNICIPALITE
La vice-présidente   La secrétaire

Maria-Chrystina Cuendet   Corinne Martin

Avenue du Prieuré 2 Case postale 63 1009 Pully Tél. 021/721 31 23 Fax 021/721 31 15
www.pully.ch - E-mail: municipalite@pully.ch

Letter of condolence from the Pully municipality

A royal audience granted to the Lausanne Mayor,
Daniel Brélaz, along with the author

Presentation of gifts offered by the City of Lausanne and the *Confrérie des Pirates d'Ouchy*, represented by two of its members, Daniel Brélaz and the author

The Lausanne delegation takes leave after the private audience that was granted

Next pages:

The Joe Louis traditional Puppet Troupe in Lausanne, 4 June 2008, during a performance in honour and in memory of HRH Princess Galyani Vadhana.

The traditional Thai puppets are about one and a half metre high, each fully articulated and animated by three people operating on stage (three women for each female character and three men for each male character). Movements performed simultaneously by puppets and their puppeteers are elegant and this complex choreography can only be achieved by experienced ballet dancers. The puppets portray heroes from the Thai traditional adventures that combine myth and humour. Puppeteers feel free to improvise by involving the audience. Another part of the show features a contortionist dancer portraying a puppet directed in the same manner but by a sole puppeteer.

In the past, these shows were reserved to the Court and then they became very popular. In 1996, this discipline was recognized as a national artistic interest by the King.

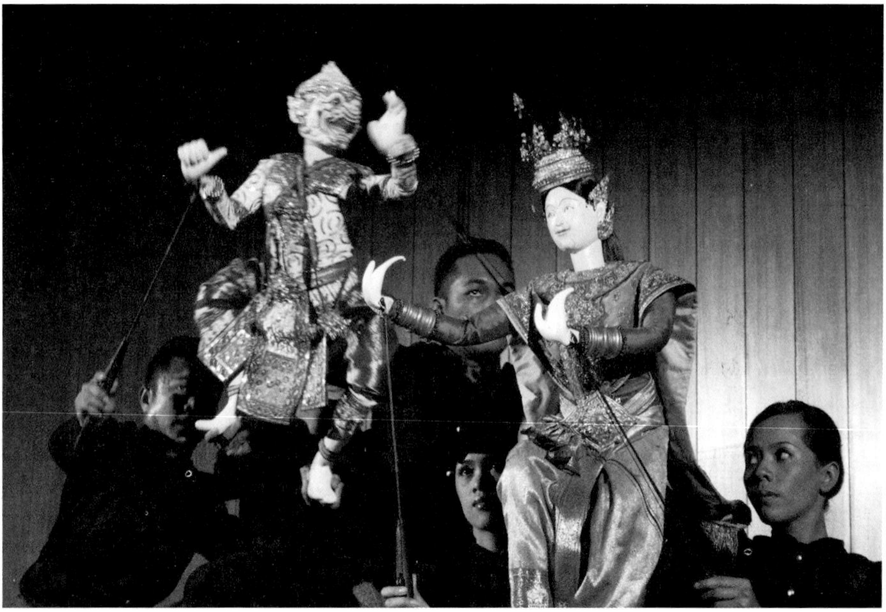

© LÉANDRE SÉRAÏDARIS

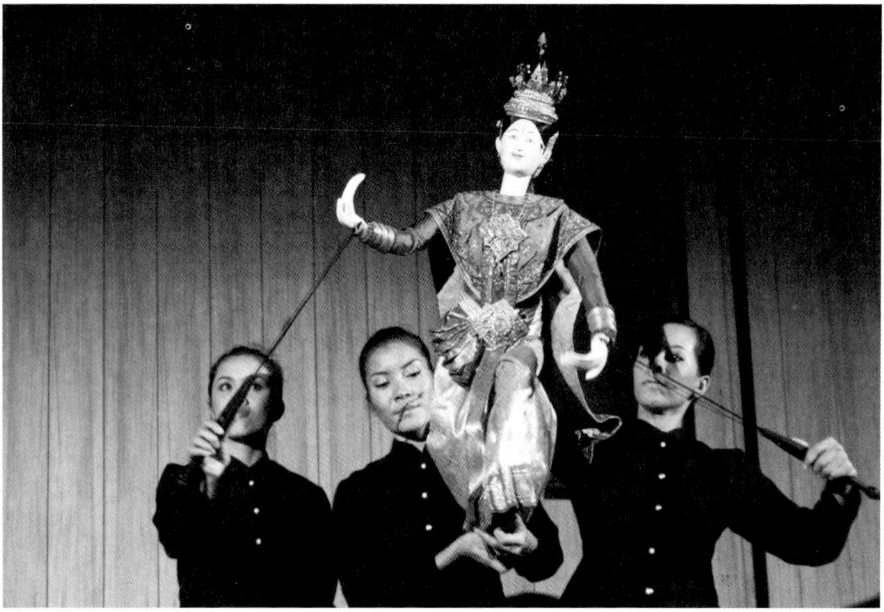

© LÉANDRE SÉRAÏDARIS

© LÉANDRE SÉRAIDARIS

© LÉANDRE SÉRAIDARIS

SECOND PART

PERENNIALITY OF PRIVILEGED RELATIONSHIPS WITH LAUSANNE AND THE COUNTRY OF VAUD

20

THE ROYAL PAVILION
OFFERED TO THE CITY OF LAUSANNE

In 1996 His Majesty the King expressed his wish to offer to the City of Lausanne a magnificent Pavilion as a souvenir of the Royal Family's stay there, so that all future visitors could see and understand the close attachment of the longest reigning sovereign of the 20th century has had with the City of Lausanne and the Canton of Vaud. The gift was to be presented in 1999, at the auspicious occasion of the King's sixth cycle celebration, that is to say his seventy-second birthday. It was a logical consequence to the celebration of His Majesty's fifty years on the throne.

Moreover, in 1997, to celebrate the centenary of the Great King Rama V's visit to Switzerland, the President of the Swiss Confederation, Arnold Koller, went to Bangkok. Each of the two Heads of State wrote a preface to a commemorative book detailing this historic visit. The preface of His Majesty the King of Thailand said, in substance, that as a result of the links that the two nations had established over these one hundred years, *"nothing is unattainable between the Swiss and the Thai"*. President Koller's preface in turn emphasized the strong links and declared that it was the duty of the Swiss people to further strengthen these bonds of friendship over the next hundred years.

To seal this friendship, there had to be, in addition to commercial and legal agreements signed between the two countries, an exceptional gesture. This was the idea of the Royal Pavilion given to Switzerland, but more particularly to the City of Lausanne.

The custom of Siam required that, since the start of the Dynasty, when the King went about the remote provinces, a Pavilion be built to welcome him because, in the rural areas, there was not always an official building prestigious enough to honour the illustrious visitor. This was where the King would formally receive members of the local community. The Pavilion would remain after the King's departure as witness to their sovereign's visit. This ancient Siamese custom was then taken up by King Rama IX, as a souvenir of the years that he and his brother had spent in the city, as well as a symbol of the following decades of warm Swiss welcome the Royal Family had received. The City of Lausanne feels extremely proud of the presence of the Royal Pavilion, jewel of the Denantou Park.

This gift, a highly symbolic and generous gesture, was proposed to the urban district and local authorities. They enthusiastically accepted it. His Majesty had from the beginning expressed his wish of seeing this building erected at the Denantou Park, which was the best known and the most beautiful public park in Lausanne, facing a lake, according to tradition. A lake that was worthy of the gift because it was Lake Léman. Furthermore, its location happens to be only a few hundred metres distance from the Vadhana Villa at *Chemin de Chamblandes*, where the Royal Family had lived.

Despite the diplomatic intervention and good offices of HE Bernard Freymond, Ambassador of Switzerland in Bangkok at that time, there was some unintentional awkwardness, however proven, from various Lausanne stakeholders in this matter. Ambassador Freymond, who had met the King, made the City of Lausanne aware of the importance of this gesture. He was listened to at first, but probably not followed through. Then several people gave their opinion without seeming to know the background of the problem. The realization of this project came to be delayed to such an extent that the idea to present a gift to the City of Lausanne was abandoned due to the legitimate loss of patience of its illustrious donor.

Indeed, some errors on the form and in the administrative processing of the file could have made people believe that the City of Lausanne did not understand its impact. In fact, there was an obvious lack of communication from the authorities concerning the symbolism of this gift and its prestige for Lausanne and its people. Then an inadequate procedure followed, perhaps due to the unusual nature of the situation.

When the Mayor, Daniel Brélaz, was elected in 2001 the issue of the Royal Pavilion became one of his priorities. He devoted himself to trying to make up for the unintentional, but recognized, mistakes made by Lausanne. In vain. At a private discussion, he confided to the author and revealed to him the aspects of the matter that the latter suspected, without knowing the details as he had not been consulted by the previous authorities. A King's decision was not to be argued with, he could only from then on personally and deeply regret this situation.

In the month of June 2003, during a visit in Bangkok, the author had the privilege of a long private audience with His Majesty. During this conversation, the King asked his opinion on the attitude of Lausanne regarding the Pavilion issue. After having explained the origin of the *faux pas*, the author stated that he was ready to work to solve this regrettable incident with the urban district and local authorities, as long as His Majesty was not opposed to the idea.

Without the King showing any objection, the author agreed to devote himself to this matter and, as soon as he returned to Switzerland, he got in touch with Daniel Brélaz. Then, with the enthusiastic agreement of the latter, he worked voluntarily at what he therefore considered to be a duty, till the kind acceptance of His Majesty and of the Royal Government of Thailand. Finally, the construction of this exceptional monument was accomplished in the park where the King wanted this symbolic gift to be erected.

The Sandoz Family settled for a long time in the upper residential part of Denantou had ceased the lower part, the actual park, to the City of Lausanne in 1928. During the conception period of the Royal Pavilion installation, the Sandoz Family expressed their support for "this magnificent project of undeniable cultural and historical value for the reputation of

Lausanne". Mrs Nicole Landolt, the daughter of the sculptor Edouard-Marcel Sandoz, who lived in the Sandoz residence, attended the official ceremony for the end of the construction of the Pavilion. That day, she congratulated the author for his work on furthering the project.

The City of Lausanne seized the occasion to produce a video film tracing the erection of this Pavilion, the making of which was carried out in specialized workshops in Bangkok, up until the inauguration, on 17 March 2009, by Her Royal Highness Princess Maha Chakri Sirindhorn, representing His Majesty the King. This film, the proceeds of which will go to a royal charity project in Thailand, is on sale at the Tourism Office in Lausanne.

Foreword by the President of the Swiss Confederation

The development of the ties of friendship between my country and the Kingdom of Thailand is literally a hundred years old success story. The foundations were laid by the official visit to Switzerland of His Majesty Rama V, King of Siam, in 1897. Over the last hundred years, these bilateral relations have been decisively influenced by the Royal Thai Dynasty to whom I pay tribute for their profound attachment to my country.

It is a particular honour for me as President of the Swiss Confederation to visit officially the Kingdom of Thailand during this commemorative year, confirming the excellent relations between our two countries which are so close to each other though belonging to different regions of our world.

The present book which we owe to Mr. Agathon Aerni demonstrates, by retracing some decisive years of Swiss-Thai relations, that a special relationship between countries in the true meaning of the word depends upon mutually enriching contacts in the political, cultural and economic fields. Hence the role of individuals and of institutions such as the Swiss School in Bangkok will remain in the future as important as it has been in the past. It will be the grateful task for our governments to strengthen this friendship even more over the next hundred years.

A. Koll

Arnold Koller,
President of the Swiss
Confederation (1997)

ALL RIGHTS RESERVED

Foreword

I am pleased that, on this historic occasion of the 100th Anniversary of the Visit to Switzerland of His Majesty King Chulalongkorn of Siam, the account of the origin of Thai-Swiss relations has been documented in a book to commemorate the event.

Thailand and Switzerland have long enjoyed a close friendship and there could hardly be a better time than this centennial moment to look back with fond memory at the historic events that had shaped our healthy relations. Such wholesome relationship, epitomizing the East-West harmony, is evident in numerous areas of endeavor, which through the passage of time could be further enhanced to greater benefit of our two peoples. But time alone could not determine the fruits of friendship; inspiration and joint efforts are much needed to galvanize the relations of nations and the affinities of people. I am therefore hopeful that the years ahead and the path towards a second centenary will be paved with greater inspiration, confidence and cooperation. I know that between us, the Thai and the Swiss, nothing is unattainable.

On this happy note, I take pleasure in welcoming the President of the Confederation of Switzerland. His official visit to Thailand in November 1997 will complete the cycle of the high-level exchange of visits between the two countries, thus reinforcing the bond of friendship between Thailand and Switzerland.

Chitralada Villa,
Dusit Palace,
Bangkok, 9th October, B.E. 2540 (1997).

Preface to the book commemorating the centenary of King Rama V's visit

384

The King grants a private audience to the author at Klai Kang Won Palace

Canton of Vaud
The Head of the Department of Safety and Environment

Mr Lysandre Séraïdaris

Lausanne, 26 August 2003

Dear Sir,

I was informed by Mr Pierre-Alain Uberti, Vice Chancellor, that you have taken over responsibility for the project concerning the construction of a Thai Pavilion in Lausanne.

While rejoicing at the news, I would like to confirm my full support for this great project whose realization will remind the people of Lausanne of the esteem and the deep mutual respect that mark our good relations with the Thai Royal Family.

I am convinced that you will lead this project to an excellent conclusion and I thank you in advance for the efforts you will make to ensure its success.

Yours sincerely,

Jean-Claude Mermoud

Translation of the document of the right page

CANTON DE VAUD

LE CHEF DU DEPARTEMENT DE LA SECURITE ET DE L'ENVIRONNEMENT
Pl. du Château 1   1014 Lausanne
Tél. 021/316 45 00   fax 021/316 45 11

Monsieur
Lysandre Seraïdaris

1009 Pully

Lausanne, le 26 août 2003

Monsieur le Directeur,

J'ai été informé par M. le Vice-chancelier Pierre-Alain Uberti que vous repreniez sous votre responsabilité le projet relatif à la construction d'un pavillon thaï sur sol vaudois, à Lausanne.

Tout en me réjouissant de cette nouvelle, je vous confirme mon plein soutien pour ce beau projet dont la réalisation rappellera à la population l'estime et le profond respect mutuels dont sont empreintes les relations du Peuple vaudois avec la Famille royale thaïlandaise.

Je suis convaincu que vous saurez mener ce projet à son bon terme et vous remercie d'ores et déjà pour tous les efforts que vous aurez fournis afin d'en garantir la réussite.

Veuillez croire, Monsieur le Directeur, à l'assurance de mes sentiments distingués.

Jean-Claude Mermoud

vaud2003.ch   1803-2003 naissance d'un canton confédéré

Testimony of the interest and support of Vaud cantonal authorities
for the construction project of a Royal Pavilion
donated to the City of Lausanne

(City of Lausanne)
General Administration and Finance
The Mayor

Mr Lysandre Séraïdaris

Lausanne, 21 February 2008

Dear Sir,

We enclose herewith a letter for the attention of His Majesty the King of Thailand to express our gratitude for the gift of the Royal Pavilion to the City of Lausanne.

We also take this opportunity to express our appreciation for the dedication and unconditional perseverance you have shown since the summer of 2003 to achieve the successful completion of this project.

It is certain that without your loyalty and personal commitment to His Majesty King Bhumibol, as well as your continual availability, this project in Denantou Park would not have been realized and Lausanne would not have the opportunity to boast about this unique monument.

Although your role in this matter was raised during my public speech of 28 September 2007, I take this opportunity to reiterate my thanks and appreciation.

We thank you in advance for conveying the enclosed letter to Mr Vajarodaya for His Majesty the King of Thailand.

Yours sincerely,

Daniel Brélaz,
Mayor of Lausanne

Translation of the document of the right page

administration générale et finances

le syndic

Monsieur **Lysandre Seraidaris**
Avenue Verdeil 22
1005 **Lausanne**

DB/gp

Lausanne, le 21 février 2008

Monsieur,

Nous vous transmettons ci-joint un courrier à destination de Sa Majesté le Roi de Thaïlande, en remerciements d'avoir fait cadeau à la Ville de Lausanne de ce Pavillon Royal.

Nous saisissons l'occasion de vous exprimer également notre reconnaissance pour le dévouement et la persévérance inconditionnelle que vous avez démontrée depuis l'été 2003 pour arriver à l'aboutissement heureux de ce projet.

Il est certain que sans votre loyauté et votre engagement personnel envers Sa Majesté le Roi Bhumibol aussi bien que votre disponibilité permanente, ce projet n'aurait pas vu le jour au parc Denantou et Lausanne ne pourrait pas s'enorgueillir de ce monument exceptionnel.

Bien que votre rôle dans cette affaire ait été relevé lors de mon allocution publique du 28 septembre 2007, je tenais à vous en réitérer les termes par la présente.

En vous remerciant par avance de bien vouloir transmettre notre lettre ci-jointe à Monsieur Vajarodaya pour Sa Majesté le Roi de Thaïlande, je vous prie d'agréer, cher Monsieur, mes salutations distinguées.

Daniel Brélaz
Syndic de Lausanne

Hôtel de Ville
place de la Palud 2
case postale 6904
CH-1002 Lausanne
tél. 4121 315 22 00

© PRIVATE COLLECTION

The City of Lausanne thanks the author for assistance to the
construction project of a Royal Pavilion
donated to the City of Lausanne

Next pages:

Unveiling ceremony of the Royal Pavilion at Denantou Park, Lausanne, 17 March 2009, by HRH Princess Maha Chakri Sirindhorn representing the King

391

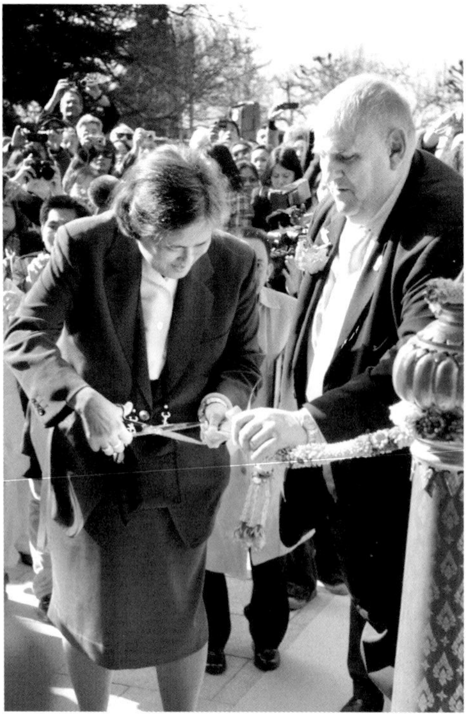

© LÉANDRE SÉRAÏDARIS

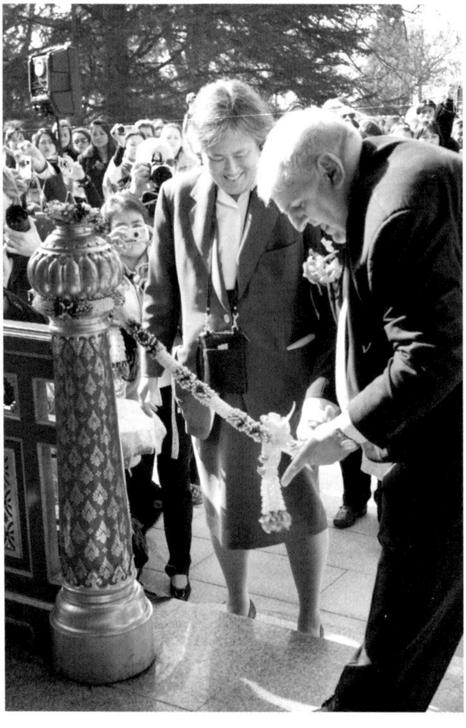

© LÉANDRE SÉRAÏDARIS

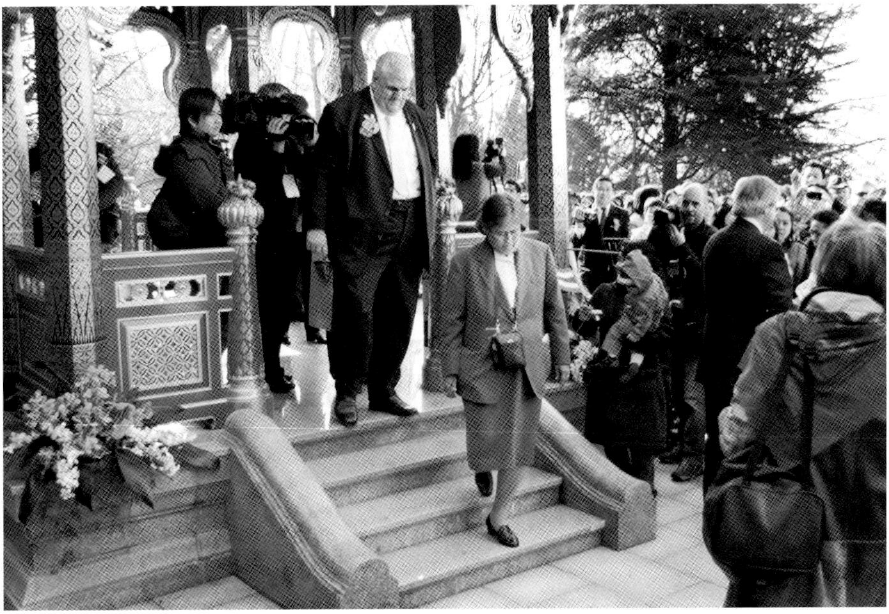

© LÉANDRE SÉRAÏDARIS

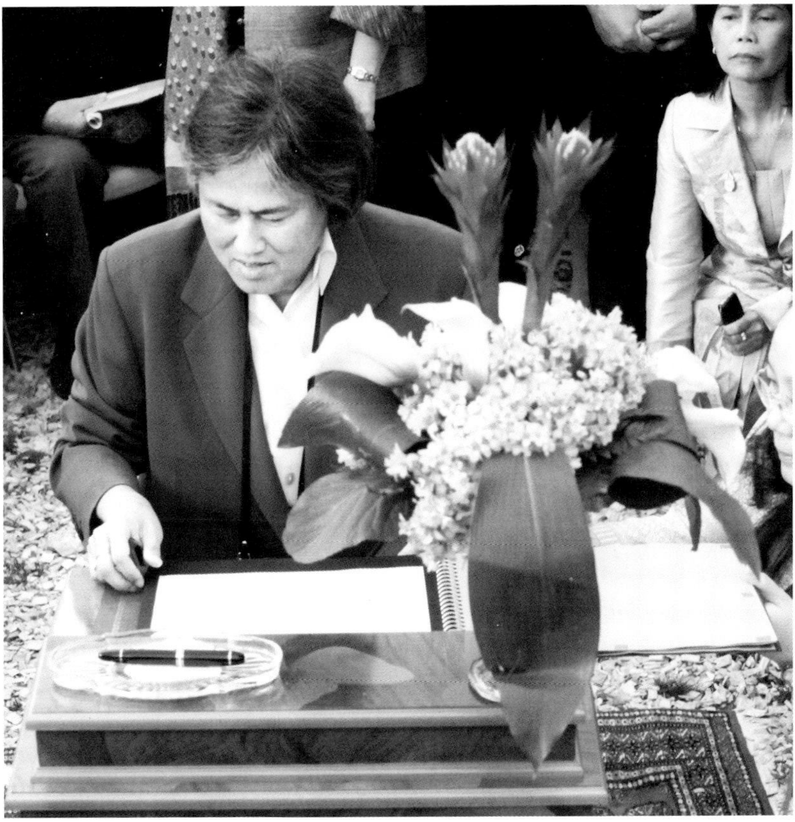

© LÉANDRE SÉRAÏDARIS

In the background, Mr Thierry Piccard,
son of Mr Jacques Piccard and friend of the author

Presentation of the offerings from the Thai community in Lausanne
for the Princess's good works

HRH Princess Maha Chakri Sirindhorn and Mrs Marie-Ange Brélaz

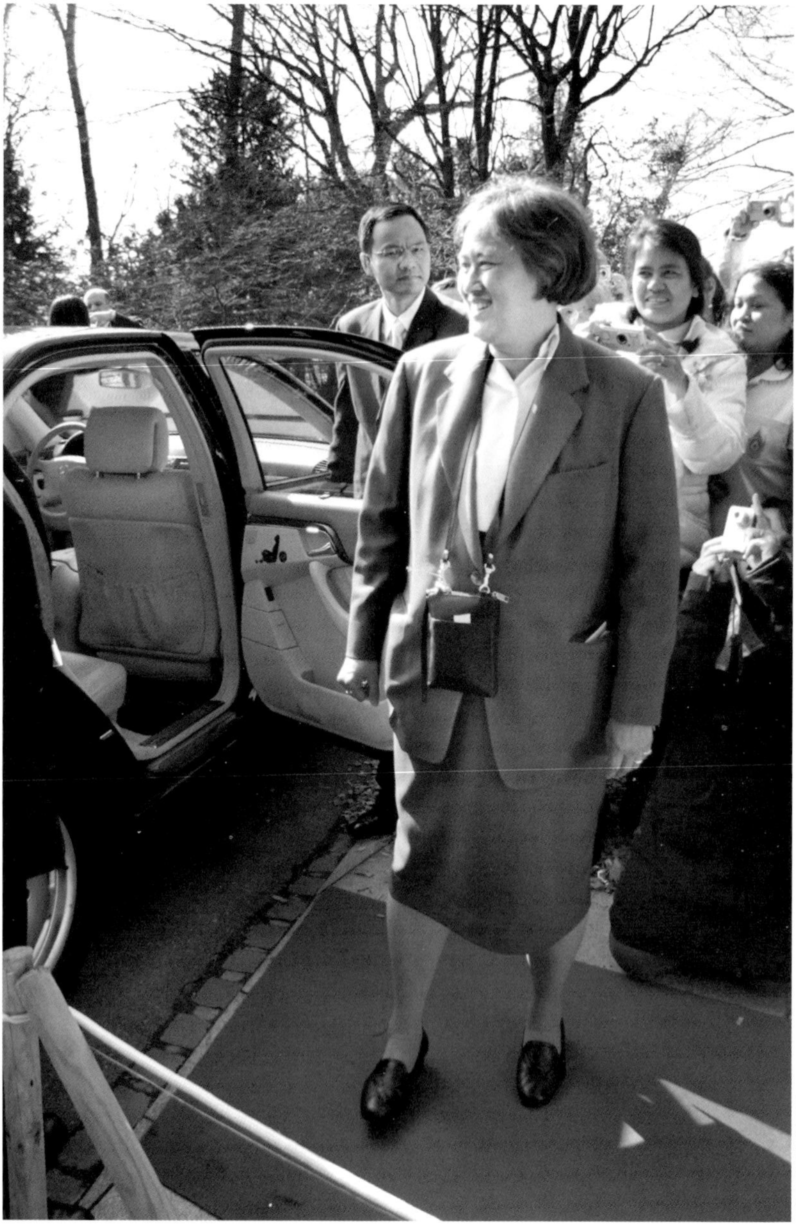

Traditional danses for the inauguration of the Pavilion

Next pages:

*The Royal Pavilion construction ending ceremony
at Denantou Park, Lausanne, 28 September 2007,
in the presence of HE Khun Khwankeo Vajarodaya and
HE Dr Chaiyong Satjipanon, Ambassador of Thailand in Bern*

HE Khun Khwankeo Vajarodaya; HE Dr Chaiyong Satjipanon; the author and Mrs Véronique Séraïdaris. In the background: Mr Jacques Mayer; Mr Daniel Brélaz; Mr Jean-René Mermoud, lawyer; and Mr Thomas Perdios

Mr Jacques Piccard, a friend of HM the King,
in conversation with the author

Mr Christian Zutter, City of Lausanne municipal Secretary; the author;
Mr Albert Modoux, architect of *Parcs et Promenades* of the City of
Lausanne and Head of the Pavilion's construction site;
Mr Daniel Brélaz; HE Dr Chaiyong Satjipanon

Mr Fabien Loï Zedda, Ouchy Mayor,
representing the *Confrérie des Pirates d'Ouchy*

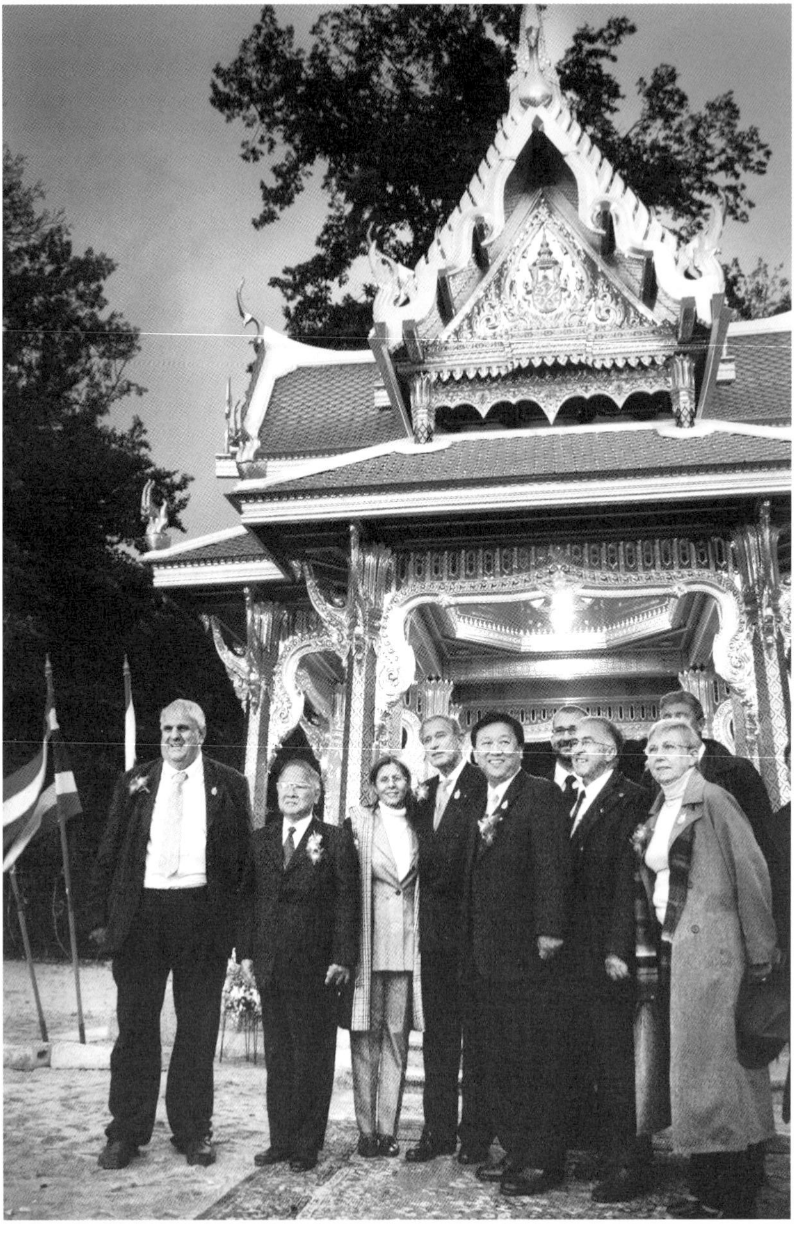

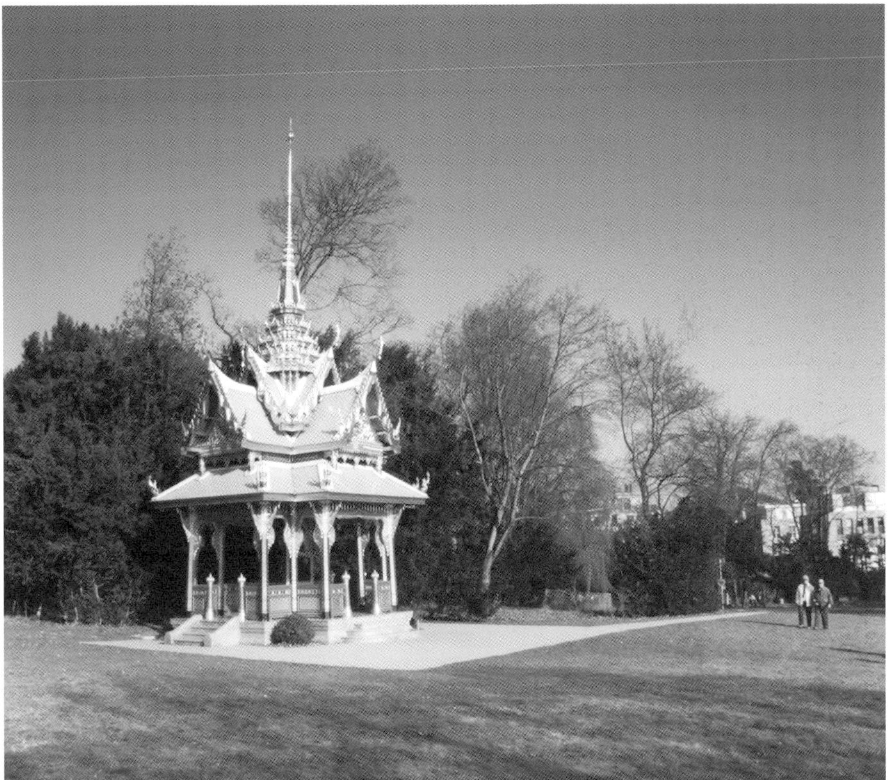

© LÉANDRE SÉRAÏDARIS

21

THE *CONFRÉRIE DU GUILLON* RECEIVED IN BANGKOK

In the Canton of Vaud is one of the oldest and most important wine-growing traditions of Switzerland, having magnificently moulded its landscape through the centuries and the origins of which went back to the beginning of the Christian era.

In order to celebrate this ancient cultural inheritance and to promote its products, the wine growers of the Canton of Vaud founded in 1954, on the model of the merchant guilds of the Middle Ages, the Brotherhood of Guillon. A *guillon* is a wooden spigot plugged in the maturing barrel used to sample wine. Members of the Brotherhood are called Companions and according to their importance, inducted personalities can receive titles of rank such as Major Companion, Jury Companion, or exceptionally, Honorary Companion.

Every year the Brotherhood gather for the solemn investiture of new Companions at Chillon Castle, a medieval fortress built on the banks of Lake Léman during the Dukes of Savoy period. New Companions are invited to swear an oath of loyalty before the Governor of Guillon. They then receive as proof of their promise a green ribbon adorned with an emblem of the Brotherhood. The Honorary Companions receive a gold ribbon. The ceremony is followed by a festive celebration, the *ressat*, traditional name of the meal served at the end of the grape harvest. There are more than four thousand Companions, in Switzerland and worldwide, including many prominent figures in the political and diplomatic field, giving the Brotherhood prestige as a recognized institution.

In the autumn of 2007, the author, himself an Honorary Companion, approached the King to request him taking membership of the Brotherhood with the highest rank of Honorary Companion. This was intended as a sign of thanks to the King for having given the Royal Pavilion to the City of Lausanne. This nomination seemed appropriate as the King had appreciated his stay in the vineyards of Lavaux in 1960, where he even visited the wine growers of Epesses with whom he had had relationships marked by a real interest for their profession. The ceremony would exceptionally take place in Bangkok, because the King no longer travels out of his Kingdom since the past forty years.

The Governor of the Brotherhood, Philippe Gex, Mayor of the wine-growing municipality of Yvorne and friend of the author was ready to accompany a delegation. All that remained was to invite other personalities of the Canton of Vaud to join in this pleasant expedition.

However, the sudden worsening of the state of health of Princess Galyani Vadhana Krom Luang Naradhiwas Rajanagarindra, in November 2007, required that the project be suspended, and her death announced, on 2 January 2008, resulted in it being put off temporarily, because the King and the entire country were in mourning.

In February 2009 the period of mourning and funeral being completed, the author presented another official request to His Majesty that the investiture take place. The request was favourably received. The author then decided to organize a delegation of personalities of the Canton of Vaud.

A date for the arrival of the delegates to the investiture was fixed for Easter 2009 which would allow the Mayor of Lausanne to be present despite urgent matters and a very full program at this period. The Governor of the Brotherhood was also available.

The delegation should have included other eminent political and economical representatives of the Canton of Vaud.

Two incidents occurred which changed plans and altered the arrangements a few days before departure. Firstly, riots by opponents of the Government of Thailand took place in central Bangkok, as was reported by the world media. Many members of the delegation then started to have doubts about the possibility of keeping the departure date. Being responsible for the delegation, the author reassured them, as he was in permanent contact with the Thai authorities.

Secondly, shortly before departure, while the author had booked the flight for almost all the participants, the Palace requested that the trip be postponed for about two weeks since the King was not available.

It was not possible either for the Governor of the Brotherhood nor for the Mayor of Lausanne to put off this trip for the investiture to an unspecified date. Other members of the delegation were informed. This called the ceremony into question as it would be once again very difficult to coordinate due to the overloaded timetables of each of the members of the delegation.

At a telephone call received the day before the anticipated departure, the Palace asked for a new date to be fixed and was informed that it was not possible to find one for the time being. After consultation with the Palace, the Grand Chamberlain called back the author in the evening to announce to him that, considering the difficulties brought about by the postponement, it was better that the trip should be maintained. Nevertheless, the delegation had to be prepared to wait for a few days in Bangkok.

The Mayor of Lausanne, who received a call in the late evening, immediately agreed to leave the next day in the morning at 8 p.m. The Thai Ambassador, HE Dr Chaiyong Satjipanon, naturally confirmed his presence to officially escort the delegation. As for the Governor of Guillon, he left the same day but took the evening flight. However, it was not possible to contact other members approached to form this delegation as the various calls and consultations had lasted until late in the evening.

As this had been considered before departure, the delegation had to wait several days before they could be received by His Majesty. They took advantage of this wait by making an official visit to the Ministry of Foreign Affairs and to the City Hall of Bangkok, to discuss ongoing joint projects.

On 21 April, at Hua Hin Palace, the ritual investiture of His Majesty to Honorary Companion of the Brotherhood of Guillon took place at a ceremony broadcast by Thai Television.

Your Majesty,

The Brotherhood of Guillon and the entire Country of Vaud, through our delegation, feels great honour and are privileged in welcoming Your Majesty to the title of Honorary Companion of our Brotherhood.

This gesture as accepted by Your Majesty shows and reinforces the privileged bonds that exist between Your Majesty and our country, Switzerland.

The Thai Pavilion most graciously given by your Majesty to the City of Lausanne stands as a real sign of the exceptional and long friendship between Thailand and Switzerland.

The gold ribbon and the golden brooch emblem of the Brotherhood are reserved for the most distinguished Swiss personalities. We are happy that Your Majesty is part of it from now on.

Please allow, Your Majesty, that this oak barrel with your name on puts a permanent seal on these privileged relations with the Canton of Vaud.

After this speech, the Governor of the Brotherhood, the Grand Chamberlain and the author came forward and the Governor kneeled before the King to offer him the gold ribbon of the Honorary Companion and the golden brooch representing a *guillon*, emblem of the Brotherhood, as well as a 25 litres oak barrel made according to tradition by one of the last craftsmen coopers still active in Switzerland.

During this trip, the Grand Chamberlain, HE Khun Khwankeo Vajarodaya, invited the guests to visit Klai Kang

Won School near Hua Hin Palace, 150 miles south of Bangkok. Upon the King's initiative, this school broadcasts by satellite, free of charge, lessons of the main teaching subjects, intended for students in the areas lacking teachers. These lessons can also be followed by expatriate Thai students and those in the neighbouring countries who are faced with the same problem of lack of schools and teachers in the remote regions.

The school is entirely funded by the Rajaprajanugroh Foundation and has established a partnership with the University of Oregon in the United States for the broadcasting of English courses by videoconference.

In collaboration with HE Khun Khwankeo Vajarodaya, the author started in 2009 a similar partnership project for the broadcasting of French lessons with the *École Nouvelle de la Suisse Romande (ENSR)* in Lausanne where both King Rama VIII and King Rama IX studied. In the first years, the ENSR started by engaging voluntary teachers on the spot for a few weeks. This cooperation is much appreciated by the management and especially by the Klai Kang Won students.

HE Khun Khwankeo Vajarodaya welcomes the Lausanne Mayor, Daniel Brélaz, and the author. All three of them are Honorary Companions of the *Confrérie du Guillon*

Khun Thaanit Vajarodaya; Lysandre C. Séraïdaris; HE Khun Khwankeo Vajarodaya; Governor Philippe Gex; and HE Dr Chaiyong Satjiparon in front of the gift that will be offered to the King during the investiture ceremony

The Governor carries out HM the King's investiture in the rank of Honorary Companion of the *Confrérie du Guillon*

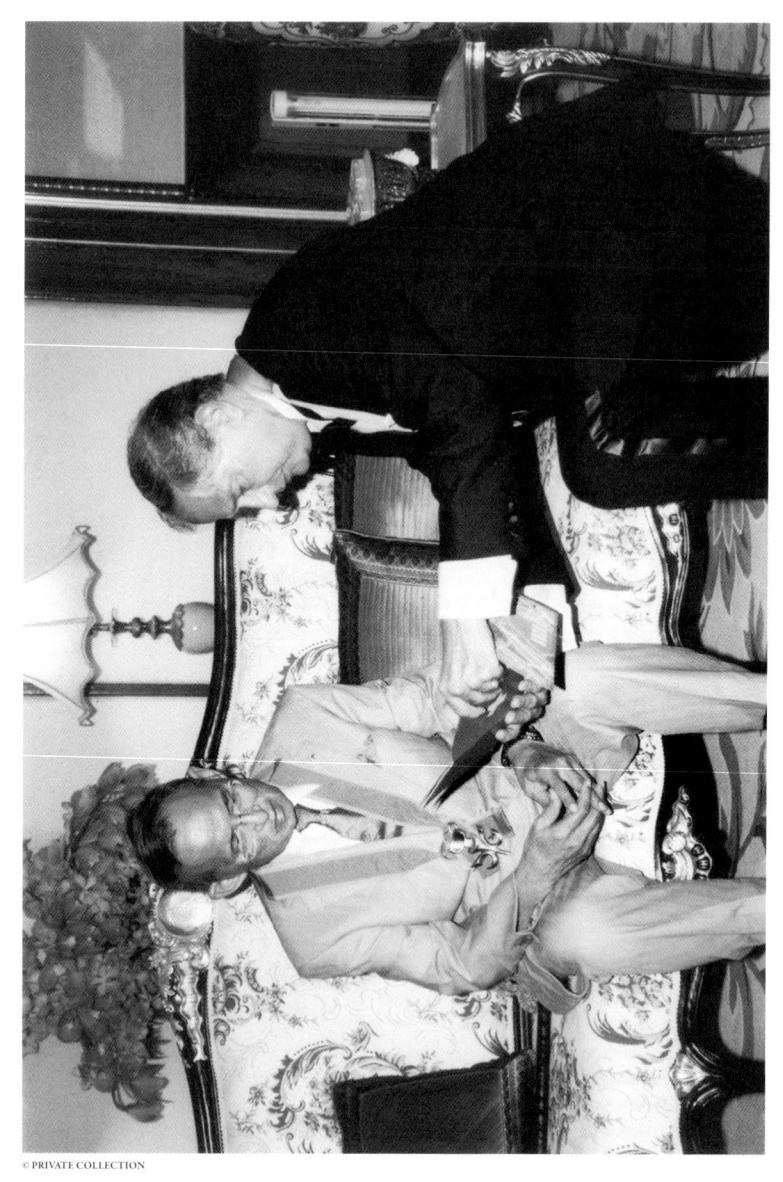

The author gives His Majesty a copy of the *Passeport lausannois*,
the first touristic brochure of the City of Lausanne representing the Royal Pavilion

© PRIVATE COLLECTION

Governor Philippe Gex and Lysandre C. Séraïdaris surround the sovereign, along with HE Khun Khwankeo Vajarodaya, for the official souvenir photo of the King's investiture

© PRIVATE COLLECTION

The Vaud delegation visits the Foundation for Distance Learning, headed by HE Khun Khwankeo Vajarodaya…

...and participates with interest in the educational programme broadcast live on this occasion

Toasts are proposed to the success of relations
between Switzerland and Thailand

Ceremony for the presentation of souvenirs of this visit

HE Khun Khwankeo Vajarodaya welcomes the Lausanne delegation at his residence of Wattana's Place, near Don Muang

22

LAUSANNE – BANGKOK, SISTER CITIES

Another project prepared by Mayor Daniel Brélaz and the author with the Bangkok Governor, M.R. Sukhumbhand Paribatra, King Rama IV's grandson, was to see Lausanne and Bangkok agree on a concept of sister cities, due to the unique relationships between the capital cities of Thailand and of the Canton of Vaud.

The project progressed well during 2009 and on 28 December 2009 Daniel Brélaz, Mayor of Lausanne, returned to Bangkok with the author, accompanied by HE Dr Chaiyong Satjipanon, Thai Ambassador in Bern, to sign the Fraternity Agreement in the presence of HE Mrs Christine Schraner-Burgener, Swiss Ambassador, as well as many Thai officials.

Signed on 29 December 2009, the Fraternity Agreement brought together the two cities to develop exchanges in the fields of education, culture, sports, environment and tourism.

* * *

**Accord de fraternité
entre
La Ville de Lausanne
Capitale du Canton de Vaud
Confédération Helvétique
et
La Ville de Bangkok
Royaume de Thaïlande**

La Ville de Lausanne, Capitale du Canton de Vaud, Confédération Helvétique et La Ville de Bangkok, Royaume de Thaïlande, acceptent par la présente de conclure un Accord de fraternité.

Le but de cet accord entre Lausanne, Ville où Sa Majesté le Roi de Thaïlande a fait ses études et Bangkok, Capitale de la Thaïlande, est de développer la compréhension et les relations amicales, afin que les deux villes en tirent un bénéfice mutuel.

Les deux parties tenteront d'établir une collaboration plus étroite dans différents secteurs d'intérêt commun, à savoir, entre autres, l'éducation, la culture, le tourisme, les sports et l'environnement.

Cet accord a été conclu à Bangkok, Royaume de Thaïlande, le 29 Décembre 2009 en deux copies originales, soit en langue française et en langue thaïe, également authentiques. Il entrera en vigueur dès la date de signature.

(M.R. Sukhumbhand Paribatra)
Gouverneur de Bangkok

(Mr. Daniel Brélaz)
Syndic de Lausanne

ข้อตกลงว่าด้วยการสถาปนาความสัมพันธ์เมืองพี่เมืองน้อง
ระหว่างเมืองโลซาน สมาพันธรัฐสวิส
และกรุงเทพมหานคร ราชอาณาจักรไทย

เมืองโลซาน แห่งสมาพันธรัฐสวิส และกรุงเทพมหานคร แห่งราชอาณาจักรไทย มีความประสงค์จะสถาปนาความสัมพันธ์เมืองพี่เมืองน้อง

ข้อตกลงความเป็นเมืองพี่เมืองน้องระหว่างเมืองโลซานซึ่งเป็นเมืองที่พระบาทสมเด็จ พระเจ้าอยู่หัวภูมิพลอดุลยเดชทรงศึกษา กับกรุงเทพมหานครซึ่งเป็นเมืองหลวง ของประเทศไทย มีวัตถุประสงค์เพื่อพัฒนาความเข้าใจอันดีและความสัมพันธ์อันดีเกิดประโยชน์ ระหว่างทั้งสองฝ่ายด้วย

เมืองโลซานและกรุงเทพมหานครจะดำเนินการพัฒนาและส่งเสริมความร่วมมือ กับอย่างใกล้ชิดในด้านต่างๆ เช่น การศึกษา วัฒนธรรม การท่องเที่ยวและการกีฬาและ สิ่งแวดล้อม

ข้อตกลงฉบับนี้ทำขึ้น ณ กรุงเทพมหานคร เมื่อวันที่ 29 ธันวาคม 2552 ประกอบด้วยข้อความทำนายไทยและภาษาฝรั่งเศส ซึ่งกฎสองฝ่ายต่างก็เห็นชอบด้วยทั้ง โดยมีผลบังคับใช้นับแต่วันที่ลงนาม

(นายแดเนียล เบรลาซ)
นายกเทศมนตรีเมืองโลซาน

(ม.ร.ว. สุขุมพันธุ์ บริพัตร)
ผู้ว่าราชการกรุงเทพมหานคร

Translation :

Fraternity Agreement
between
the City of Lausanne, capital of the Canton of Vaud, Swiss Confederation
and
the City of Bangkok, Kingdom of Thailand

The City of Lausanne, capital of the Canton of Vaud, Swiss Confederation, and the City of Bangkok, Kingdom of Thailand, hereby agree to enter into a Fraternity Agreement.

The purpose of this Agreement between the City of Lausanne, where His Majesty the King of Thailand has studied, and Bangkok, capital of Thailand, is to develop understanding and friendly relations for the mutual benefit of the two cities.

Both cities will endeavour to establish closer cooperation in various areas of common interest, including, inter alia, education, culture, sports, environment and tourism.

This Agreement was signed in Bangkok, Kingdom of Thailand on December 29, 2009, in two original copies, in French and Thai, equally authentic. It shall enter into force on the date of signature.

Mr Daniel Brélaz
Mayor of Lausanne

M.R.Sukhumbhand Paribatra
Governor of Bangkok

Other links between the two cities concern distinctions conferred on HE Khwankeo Vajarodaya in honour of the Royal Family.

He received, on 18 June 2010, the title of Honorary Professor from the *École Hôtelière de Lausanne* which was conferred upon him for his unique professional career among the alumni of this prestigious institution.

Indeed, because of his brilliant studies in this institution at the end of the 1940s, HE Khwankeo Vajarodaya became Head of the Thai Royal Household and thereby had the chance to get to know the most renowned Chefs of high standard gastronomy. He therefore obtained the highest honour of being appointed Honorary President of the Chefs des Chefs Club (CCC) which gathers Chefs of the Heads of State of several countries.

As another distinction awarded to the Grand Chamberlain in the perspective of strengthening the relationships between Thailand and the capital of the Canton of Vaud was to promote him to the rank of Honorary Companion of the Brotherhood of Guillon for having mentioned the Country of Vaud's wines in the chapters of his famous book *"The Evolution and Art of Setting Tables, Catering, Beverages and Menus"*. The ceremony took place at the Chillon Castle as per the tradition.

Diploma of Honorary President of the Chefs des Chefs Club conferred on HE Khun Khwankeo Vajarodaya by this very exclusive institution

Diploma of Honorary Professor from the prestigious *École Hôtelière de Lausanne* conferred on HE Khun Khwankeo Vajarodaya in honour of his efforts in promoting the profession throughout his career

HRH Princess Maha Chakri Sirindhorn visiting the Rolex Learning Centre of the *École polytechnique fédérale de Lausanne (EPFL)*, along with the author; she's welcomed by Professor Dr Francis-Luc Perret, Vice-President of the *EPFL*

During an investiture ceremony at Chillon Castle, HE Khun
Khwankeo Vajarodaya was made Honorary Companion of the
Confrérie du Guillon. He's surrounded by his godfathers: the author
and Mr Philippe Gex, Yvorne Mayor and Brotherhood Governor

EPILOGUE

Cléon Séraïdaris, along with the Princess Mother, was entrusted with the historical privilege of teaching and guiding a young man who was to become the beloved respected sovereign of more than sixty million Thai and who earned the highest esteem of the entire international community for his total dedication to his Kingdom.

At a long private audience, King Rama IX confided to the author how deeply attached he and his brother, King Rama VIII, had been to their tutor, and thus wanted to express his gratitude to the son of this tutor who has taught him so much.

His Majesty's words were received by the author with great emotion and will remain forever in his memory and in his heart.

Lausanne and Bangkok, 2011

ACKNOWLEDGEMENTS

The author wishes to express his sincere gratitude to all those who supported him in accomplishing this work.

Especial thanks go to the Thai Royal Household who graciously contributed photographs to complete his private collection and to Khun Thaanit Vajarodaya whose precious advice was of invaluable support.

Immense gratitude goes to Léandre Séraïdaris, son of the author, for his unfailing support in restoring original documents, producing more recent photographs and realizing the layout for this book, as well as to Françoise Riette for her availability and meticulous proof-reading of the French version of this book.

Sincere thanks to Dr Adithep Venuchandra for the translation into Thai language and thank to Kru Rernchai Thonglor (Thai language expert from Chitralada School) for his thorough proofreading, and thanks to Dr Jindarat Jumsai Na Ayudhya for the translation to English as well as to Jane Liardon and George Convelle-Brent for their excellent proof-reading of the English version.

INDEX

NAMES OF MEMBERS OF THE ROYAL FAMILY

Bee: p. 57.
Chakri Dynasty: p. 157.
Choonhavan Boonruen: p. 16, 17.
Choonhavan Chartchai: p. 16.
Crown Prince Maha Vajiralongkorn: p. 32, 264, 265, 285, 299.
Great King Chulalongkorn: p. 32, 37, 356.
King Ananda: p. 26, 32, 52, 57, 58, 59, 62, 74, 77, 85, 88, 92, 98, 99, 100, 101, 105, 106, 107, 121, 122, 134, 135, 137, 140, 141, 143, 146, 149, 150, 151, 152, 155, 157, 161, 164, 167, 187, 354.
King Bhumibol Adulyadej: p. 33.
King Mongkut: p. 189.
King Prajadhipok: p. 32.
King Rama IV: p. 51, 189, 423.
King Rama V: p. 32, 37, 51, 356, 379, 384.
King Rama VI: p. 32.
King Rama VII: p. 32, 52, 230.
King Rama VIII: p. 13, 21, 32, 80, 118, 156, 159, 166, 171 – 175, 188, 230, 410.
King Rama IX: p. 13, 21, 33, 121, 157, 177, 223 – 245, 380, 410, 431.
King Vajiravudh: p. 32, 353.
Kittiyakara Sirikit: p. 193.
Lek: p. 57, 97, 102, 103, 105, 155.
Mahidol Ananda: 26, 99, 100.
Mahidol Bhumibol (or Pumipol): p. 24, 52, 57, 99, 132, 158, 175.
Mahidol Galyani Vadhana: p. 57, 101.
Mahidol Sangwal: p. 28, 33, 51, 132, 133, 156, 353.
May: p. 353.
Monkey (The): p. 104, 106.

Nant: p. 57, 97, 100, 102, 155.
Prince Ananda: p. 52.
Prince Bhumibol: p. 57, 58, 59, 73, 74, 85, 86, 92, 98, 121, 123, 139, 141, 156, 157, 167, 187.
Prince Birabongse Bhanudej Bhanubandh; Prince Bira; Bira: p. 188,189, 190, 191, 198, 199, 200, 201, 202, 203, 204, 205, 206.
Prince Chula Chakrabongse: p. 140, 189.
Prince Mahidol of Songkla: p. 33, 51, 52, 54, 353.
Prince Rangsit: p. 247.
Prince Vichitwongwuthikrai: p. 84, 136.
Princess Chulabhorn Walailak: p. 33, 287, 303.
Princess Galyani Vadhana: p. 22, 30, 32, 52, 69, 101, 151, 155, 156, 161, 192, 229, 288, 317, 318, 337, 340, 353 – 375, 406.
Princess Maha Chakri Sirindhorn: p. 14, 33, 287, 297, 305, 318, 345, 383, 390, 395, 428.
Princess Ubolratana: p. 32, 250, 264, 287, 296, 299, 304.
Queen Sawang Wattana: p. 33.
Queen Sirikit: p. 33, 193, 224, 232, 233, 234, 239, 241, 245, 250, 258, 259, 295, 301.
Ratanakul Galyani Vadhana: p. 151.
Royal Household: p. 17, 216, 319, 426, 433.
Sornsongkram Jitat: p. 362, 363.
Sornsongkram Dhasanawalaya: p. 354, 355, 360, 362, 363.
Vichitwongwuthikrai Sae; Lady Sae; Mrs Vigit: p. 84, 100, 136.

PROPER NOUNS – THAILAND

Chanruan Sawate: p. 85.
Paribatra Sukhumbhand: p. 423.
Pramudwinai Don: p. 345.
Prija Bahiddha-Nukara, "Peter": p. 184.
Ratanakul Aram: p. 140, 141, 192, 229, 354.
Samita Pintu Rosesarin: p. 275.
Satjipanon Chaiyong: p. 275, 280, 356, 398, 399, 401, 408, 412, 423.
Satrabhaya Anek: p. 97, 110.

Vajarodaya Kaewkhwan: p. 17, 215, 219, 220, 221, 273.
Vajarodaya Khwankeo: p. 17, 19, 215, 216, 217, 218, 219, 220, 221, 275, 276, 280, 282, 319, 327, 329, 30, 333, 398, 399, 409, 410, 411, 412, 415, 416, 420, 426, 427, 429.
Vajarodaya Pensri: p. 221.
Vajarodaya Thaanit: p. 412, 433.
Vajarodaya Wattana: p. 221, 330, 333, 335.

PROPER NOUNS – SWITZERLAND

Barras Albert: p. 215.
Bosshard Rodolphe Théophile: p. 39, 48.
Brélaz Daniel: p. 13, 14, 255, 256, 275, 276, 277, 280, 281, 282, 356, 357, 366, 367, 370, 371, 381, 382, 388, 389, 399, 401, 411, 423, 424, 425.
Brélaz Marie-Ange: p. 395.
Chaudet Paul: p. 292.
Fonjallaz Gérard: p. 286.
Freymond Bernard: p. 381.
Gex Philippe: p. 406, 412, 415, 429.
Grumser André: p. 224, 232, 233, 234.
Guisan Henri: p. 57, 179.
Hersch, Miss: p. 105, 107.
Jaques Philippe: p. 59.
Kern, Mr: p. 156.
Koller Arnold: p. 379.
Landolt, Mr: p. 45.
Landolt Nicole: p. 383.
Loï Zedda Fabien: p. 401.
Mayer Jacques: p. 357, 399.
Mermoud Jean-René: p. 285, 345, 399.
Modoux Albert: p. 401.
Perret Francis-Luc: p. 428.
Petitpierre Max: p. 293.
Piccard Auguste: p. 187.
Piccard Jacques: p. 187, 200, 400, 394.
Piccard Thierry: p. 394.
Roux César: p. 38.

Rusconi Baptiste: p. 317, 318.
Rusconi, Jean-Baptiste: p. 317, 318.
Sandoz Edouard-Marcel: p. 383.
Sandoz Family: p. 382.
Scherz Family: p. 286.
Schraner-Burgener Christine: p. 423.
Secrétan Roger: p. 170.
Séraïdaris Alexandra: p. 319, 322, 329, 333, 335, 341.
Séraïdaris Léandre (Cléon's eldest son): p. 51, 190.
Séraïdaris Léandre (Cléon's grandson): p. 346, 433.
Séraïdaris Magdalena: p. 39, 48, 49, 51, 235, 318.
Suriyong Marcelle: p. 51, 308.
Suriyong Rasmi: p. 51, 52, 308.
Suriyong Surin: p. 308.
Tito (Cat): p. 97, 109, 154, 155, 178.
Zutter Christian: p. 401.

OTHER PROPER NOUNS

Armstrong Louis; "Satchmo": p. 286, 300.
Churchill Winston: p. 151.
King Farouk: p. 151.
King Frederick IX of Denmark: p. 226, 272.
Maserati brothers: p. 190, 202.
McDonald Malcolm; Sir Malcolm: p. 226, 227.
Prince Baudouin of Belgium: p. 190.
Prince Rainier of Monaco: p. 190, 200.
Prince Vittorio Emanuele of Italy: p. 190, 200.
Séraïdaris Angelos: p. 37, 40, 42, 45, 49.
Séraïdaris Constantin: p. 37, 40.
Séraïdaris Elli, known as Nelly's: p. 49.
Séraïdaris Marianthi: p. 37, 38, 40.
Séraïdaris Nicolaos: p. 37, 40, 45.
Séraïdaris Pâris: p. 37, 40, 45.
Séraïdaris Yannis: p. 37, 40, 42, 45.
Venizélos Elefthérios: p. 38, 42.
Zervoudaki Christo: p. 38, 42.
Zervoudaki Family: p. 37.

THAI PLACE NAMES

Ayutthaya: p. 328.
Bang Pa In: p. 328, 329.
Bangkok: p. 57, 72, 97, 98, 103, 104, 105, 106, 107, 158, 164, 165, 166, 172, 174, 175, 216, 218, 224, 228, 229, 250, 252, 256, 264, 265, 266, 274, 286, 287, 318, 326, 354, 356, 366, 367, 368, 369, 379, 381, 382, 383, 405, 406, 407, 408, 410, 423, 424, 425, 431.
Chao Phraya River: p. 319, 321, 332.
Chiang Mai: p. 318, 354.
Chitralada Palace: p. 254, 273, 275, 277, 278, 326.
Don Muang: p. 420.
Hua Hin: p. 21, 178, 218, 224, 262, 274, 281, 408, 410.
Kingdom of Siam: p. 37, 189.
Klai Kang Won: p. 21, 218, 262, 274, 281, 282, 385, 409, 410.
Nakhon Si Thammarat: p. 217.
Pattani: p. 354.
Pattaya: p. 191, 204.
Residence *Le Dix*: p. 318.
Sra Pathum Palace: p. 57.
Sukhumvit: p. 318.
Wat Phra Keo: p. 364.
Wat Po: p. 364.

SWISS PLACE NAMES

Adelboden: p. 71, 72, 79, 80, 81.
Arosa: p. 71, 75, 76, 77, 85, 87, 88, 89, 91, 92, 94, 95, 128, 140.
Avenue de l' Avant-Poste, Lausanne: p. 314, 361, 337.
Avenue des Mousquines, Lausanne: 38, 42.
Avenue Sainte-Luce, Lausanne: p. 38.
Avenue Tissot, Lausanne: p. 52.
Avenue de Lavaux, Pully: p. 337.
Boulevard de la Forêt, Pully: p. 337.
Bernese Oberland: p. 71, 338.
Canton of Vaud: p. 19, 71, 194, 225, 248, 272, 286, 293, 379, 386, 387, 405, 406, 407, 409, 423, 424, 425, 426.
Champex: p. 71, 77, 78.
Chemin de Chamblandes, Pully: p. 57, 110, 179, 202, 381.
Chexbres: p. 292.
Chillon Castle: p. 405, 426, 429.
Country of Vaud: p. 409, 426.
Davos: p. 71, 136, 137, 138, 141, 287.
Denantou Park, Lausanne: p. 14, 380, 382, 388, 389, 390, 398.
Epesses: p. 285, 286, 406.
Flonzaley: p. 285, 286, 287, 294, 295, 296, 297, 299, 345, 359.
Geneva: p. 149, 160, 164, 180, 187, 192, 195, 291, 353, 357.
Gstaad: p. 286, 287, 300, 301.
Lake Léman: p. 285, 298, 380, 405.
La Blécherette: p. 188, 190.
Lavaux (vineyards of): p. 406.

Monts-de-Pully: p. 179.
Morges: p. 192, 193.
Ouchy: p. 285, 298, 401.
Préverenges: p. 192.
Pully: p. 57, 122, 179, 183, 337, 342, 368, 369.
Renens: p. 151.
Route du Lac: p. 192.

Rue de la Grotte, Lausanne: p. 215.
Rue de la Tour-Maîtresse , Genève: p. 187.
Vadhana Villa: p. 57 – 69, 97, 122, 123, 126, 161, 163, 177, 178, 188, 225, 231, 240, 241, 245, 381.
Verbier: p. 355.
Yvorne: p. 406, 429.
Zurich: p. 126, 155.

OTHER PLACE NAMES

Aden: p. 101, 103, 225, 226.
Ain: p. 195.
Alexandria: p. 37.
Antibes: p. 72, 82.
Bellegarde: p. 224.
Bologna: p. 190, 202.
Bombay: p. 150.
Bonifacio, Strait of: p. 100.
Broadway: p. 71.
Bukit Serene: p. 226, 227, 252.
Cairo: p. 149, 150, 151.
Calcutta: p. 150, 151.
Cambridge, Massachusetts: p. 52.
Colombo: p. 225, 226, 227, 228, 249, 251.
Constantinople: p. 37, 38.
Crete: p. 100, 224.
Delhi: p. 150.
Dresden: p. 37, 38.
French Riviera: p. 72.
Genoa: p. 72.
Germany: p. 37, 52, 153.
Heidelberg: p. 52.
Huberstrasse, Dresden: p. 37.
Islands of the 12 Apostles: p. 103.
Indochina: p. 153.
Istanbul: p. 37.

Japan: p. 121, 153.
Karachi: p. 150, 151.
Kavála: p. 37.
Ligurian Coast: p. 72.
London: p. 52, 191, 353.
Lyon: p. 195.
Malaysia: p. 227.
Messina, Strait of: p. 100.
Monza: p. 190, 201, 203.
Nantua: p. 155, 212.
Nice: p. 224.
Oyonnax: p. 195.
Penang: p. 104.
Port Said: p. 100, 101, 102, 224, 249, 250.
Portofino: p. 83.
Portugal: p. 122.
Prague: p. 357.
Red Sea: p. 102, 103.
Singapore: p. 226, 228, 250, 252.
Spain: 122.
Stromboli: p. 100.
Suez: p. 225.
Suez, Canal: p. 100, 250.
Suez, Gulf: p. 102.
United States of America: 52, 122, 123, 152, 155, 410.
Villefranche Bay: p. 224.

OTHER NAMES – THAILAND

AS Radio: p. 216, 217, 253.
Bhubing Palace: p. 318.
Bira International Circuit: p. 191, 204, 205, 206, 207.
Chiang Mai University: p. 354.
Chulalongkorn University: p. 239, 354.

Dusit Palace: p. 216.
Foundation for Distance Learning: p. 218, 281, 416.
Hanuman: p. 189.
Joe Louis Troupe: p. 357, 373.
Kasetsart University: p. 354.

Life cycle: p. 22, 71, 72, 355, 379.
Prince of University: p. 354.
Rajaprajanugroh Foundation: p. 217, 410.
Royal Government of Thailand: p. 382.
Royal Thai Parliament: p. 152, 155.

School Milk Program: p. 272, 273, 275, 278.
Siriraj Hospital, Bangkok: p. 356.
Traditional Thai Puppet: p. 357, 373.
University of Agriculture, Bangkok: p. 158.
White Mouse: p. 189.

OTHER NAMES – SWITZERLAND

Alumni Association of the *École Nouvelle*: p. 171 – 175, 348, 349.
Automobile Grand Prix of Lausanne: p. 188, 190, 199, 200.
Bathyscaphe *Trieste*: p. 187.
Beau-Rivage Palace (Hotel), Lausanne: p. 287.
Bois-de-Vaux Cemetery: 346.
Bois-du-Moulin's Chalet, Pully: p. 183.
Canton of Vaud Security Police: p. 194, 225, 286.
Central Thesis Office, Zurich: p. 155.
Champ Soleil Primary School, Lausanne: p. 353.
Champittet College, Lausanne: p. 216, 287.
Chefs des Chefs Club (CCC): p. 426.
City of Lausanne (incl. authorities): p. 14, 288, 346, 357, 358, 371, 379, 380, 381, 382, 383, 388, 389, 401, 406, 409, 414.
Confrérie des Pirates d'Ouchy: p. 371, 401.
Confrérie du Guillon: p. 405 – 420, 429.
École Nouvelle (former name), Chailly-sur-Lausanne: p. 38, 57, 59, 65, 123, 171 – 175.
École Nouvelle de la Suisse Romande (ENSR) (current name): p. 348, 349, 410.
École Polytechnique Fédérale de Lausanne (EPFL): p. 428.
École Hôtelière de Lausanne (EHL): p. 19, 216, 426, 427.
Faculty of Law at the University of Lausanne: p. 39, 46, 47, 121, 223, 247.

Faculty of Pharmacy at the University of Lausanne: p. 353.
Feuille d'   Avis de Lausanne: p. 154.
Graduate School of Business, Lausanne: p. 216.
High School for Girls, Lausanne: p. 353.
International School of Geneva: p. 353.
International Festival of Classical Music, Verbier: p. 355.
La Clairière, Summer Camp, Arveyes: p. 129 – 133.
Miremont School, Lausanne: p. 52, 353.
Montchoisi clinic, Lausanne: p. 264.
Montchoisi skating rink, Lausanne: p. 287, 304, 305.
Patapoum Club: p. 59, 104, 106, 107, 105, 116.
Palace Hotel, Gstaad: p. 286, 300.
Palais de Beaulieu (Exhibition and Congress Site), Lausanne: p. 288.
Palais Impérial (Restaurant), Genève: p. 187.
Passeport lausannois (Touristic Brochure): p. 414.
Photo-Ciné Rich, Lausanne: p. 215.
Pully authorities: 179.
Pully municipality: p. 368, 369.
Royal Pavilion: p. 14, 379 – 403, 414.
Radio Suisse Romande: p. 216.
State of Fribourg Agricultural Institute: p 215, 273.
Swiss authorities: p. 122.
Tourism Office, Lausanne: p. 383.
Vaud cantonal authorities: p. 386, 387.
Zimmerli Institute: p. 72.

MISCELLANEOUS

Allies (The): p. 153.
"Blue Night": p. 71.
British Racing Drivers' Club (BRDC): p. 188, 206.
Daimler: p. 255, 261.
Dakota (Aeroplane): p. 150.

Delahaye: p. 187, 224, 229, 231, 255, 260, 261, 262.
English Racing Automobiles (ERA): p. 189, 198.
Fiat Topolino: p. 188, 192, 194, 209, 211.
French Government: p. 356.